Introduction to ActionScript Workbook

An introduction to ActionScript and the fundamentals of programming

My love and thanks to those who gave me their love and support.

Art

FILES FOR THE BOOK

The files for this book are available for download from:

www.ichibantraining.com/downloads

DISCOUNT PRICING

If your organization would like to purchase these books at a discount please contact the author. More information is available at www.ichibanTraining.com.

Table of Contents

CHAPTER 1 – ABOUT ACTIONSCRIPT

Overview

This chapter examines the history and some of the basics of ActionScript.

Topics

- History
- Formatting code
- Organizing code
- Naming conventions

History of ActionScript

ActionScript is the programming language used with Flash. ActionScript is based on the JavaScript (ECMAscript) language. There have been three versions of the ActionScript language.

ActionScript 1 (AS1) was limited in its abilities and did not have features such as data typing and case sensitive syntax that many developers wanted. ActionScript 2 (AS2) appeared to add many of these features in the Flash development tool. ActionScript 2 actually compiled as, and ran, as ActionScript 1 in the SWF. Performance was limited with these versions of ActionScript.

ActionScript 3 was a complete rewrite of the language. ActionScript 3 added several features that make AS3 more like Java than standard JavaScript. These features include data typed variables and class based inheritance.

To implement ActionScript 3 a new Flash player, or virtual machine, was created to run the new language. For legacy support the Flash player was rebuilt to hold two virtual machines. ActionScript Virtual Machine 1 (AVM1) runs AS1 and AS2. ActionScript Virtual Machine 2 (AVM2) runs AS3. ActionScript 3 performance in AVM2 is remarkably faster than the older versions in AVM1. AVM2 was added to Flash Player 9 in 2006.

Case sensitive

ActionScript is case sensitive. The following example is treated by ActionScript as three different names

- **aVariable**
- **AVARIABLE**
- **Avariable**

Formatting code

Related file: The following file contains the example for this discussion. [class files]/finalProject/Solution_ichibanTravel.fla.

Free form

ActionScript code can be written free form. This means ActionScript can have any amount of whitespace and be styled and formatted as the author wishes. Consistency in using a chosen style of formatting will make reading and troubleshooting code much easier.

Well formed code

Well formed code means code that is written correctly with regard to structure. Code may be well formed but have other technical errors such as misspellings, incorrect values or bad logic.

Well formed code means each opening character is matched by a closing character where needed. Statements are terminated. Expressions and statements are nested properly. No illegal characters are used.

Flash has a tool that will tell if code is well formed. It is demonstrated in the next example. Code must be well formed before it can be automatically formatted in Flash.

Whitespace

ActionScript can be formatted in many different ways. In many cases formatting comes down to a matter of personal style. Some developers prefer formatting that creates more compact code with fewer and shorter lines. The rational is that such code is easier to scroll through and search visually.

Other developers prefer formatting that aligns opening and closing curly braces. This makes it easier to be sure opening and closing are matched.

Much like HTML, white space can be used at the discretion of the author.

```
var variable1:String="Wow.";
var variable2 : String = "Wow." ;
myFunction1("argument1","argument2");
myFunction2 ( "argument1",  "argument2" ) ;
function myFunction1(arg1,arg2)
{
   trace("TAADAA");
}
function myFunction2 ( arg1, arg2 )
{
   trace ( "TAADAA" );
}
```

All of the above examples will work the same. Be cautious of white space inside of quotes, it is treated differently. White space inside of quotes is taken literally.

Code organization

ActionScript statements can be arranged in many different ways. Different methods of arrangement are suitable for projects of different complexity.

In simple projects code is often arranged by grouping together lines of code that are related.

In larger projects code is more often organized into sections where the code is grouped together by what it is doing.

Code organization in larger projects often follows the following order.

1. Variable declarations
2. Initializing variables
3. Instantiating arrays and other objects
4. Initial calls to functions
5. Assigning handlers
6. Handlers
7. Functions

Examples of both type of code organization will be used in this course.

Where to place code

Code is often placed in a special layer named actions. This layer is kept at the top of the layer stack. Only code is placed in this layer, it does not hold content. These conventions are best practices and not technical requirements.

It is common for some movieClips to carry the code that gives them functionality inside their own timelines. Again, the code is placed in a layer named actions.

Standard ActionScript can be kept in external files and compiled into an SWF by using an include statement in an actions layer. External code more formally formatted as a class file can also be used. Class based development is discussed briefly in an upcoming chapter and thoroughly covered in the course on object oriented programming (OOP).

Naming conventions

The names used are at the discretion of the developer. At the very least, names should clearly identify the element they are naming. Abbreviation is discouraged. Longer, clearer names are preferred.

The following conventions should be followed when creating names in ActionScript.

- Do not use spaces in names.
  Spaces create two words or names instead of one. Use an underscore instead of a space.
- Only use letters, numbers and the underscore. Do not use other characters in names. Intra-capitalization is preferred to separate words in names instead of the underscore.
- Use intra-capitalization (camel case) when a name is made up of two or more words. Examples: buttonHandler, myFunction, hitCount, etc.
- Do not start a name with a capital letter. Leading capital letters are used by convention to identify a special element of programming; classes.
- Do not start a name with a number.

It is a common practice to add a few letters the front of a name to identify the type of object the name represents. A movieClip might be named mcTitle, a button might be named btnHome, etc.

An older ActionScript naming convention added an underscore and identifying letters at the end of the name. For example, adding _mc for a movieClip. In older versions of Flash this provided some code hinting. Newer versions of Flash no longer use the suffixes to provide code hints. Data typing is used to provide hints in the latest version of Flash.

ActionScript editing preferences

Flash has a tool and preferences that assist programmers with formatting their code. The formatting can be changed to a number of different styles. These styles can be applied to well formed code with the click of a button.

Import statements

Classes are the blueprints that all objects in Flash come from. Many of these blueprints are built into the Flash player. Some, such as the Tweening and Easing classes used later on in this course, are not part of the player. These classes are kept external to the player to keep the download size of the player small.

When these extra classes are needed they are added to the SWF. They are made available by using import statements. They are then automatically compiled into the SWF when they are used. Imports should be the first thing in the code. This makes sure the classes are available to the rest of the code.

When working in the Actions editor some imports may be added automatically. This occurs when code completion is used to assign data types (see the next chapter). Many of the imports are not technically required when code is written in timelines. These optional imports may be kept or deleted.

Some developers like to see all imported classes declared. Others prefer to only see imports that are strictly required.

This course book and examples only use and show imports if they are strictly required.

Try it – Setting ActionScript Editing Preferences

Challenge

Explore the ActionScript editor's preferences.

There is a suggestion for solving the challenge on this page.

There is no real 'solution' to this challenge. It is intended to familiarize students with the preferences of the ActionScript editor.

An example file has been provided.

Example File

[class files]/finalProject/Solution_ichibanTravel.fla.

The example file contains the final Flash project built during this course. The final project uses many of the different projects that will be built during the class. It provides enough ActionScript to demonstrate different formatting options and other preferences.

Suggestion

1. Open the file.
2. Select frame 1 of the actions layer.
3. Open the Actions editor.
   The actions editor can be opened several ways.
   - Right click on frame 1 of the actions layer and choose actions from the menu.
   - Go to the Window menu at the top of the workspace and select Actions from the list of windows.
   - Press the F9 key (Windows).
4. Examine the code. This example contains a number of different actions. They will be explained in detail by the end of the course. They are provided to allow a discussion of the topics in this chapter.
5. In the Actions editor window press the Check syntax icon (the blue check icon at the top of the editor). Nothing should happen as the code is well formed and syntactically correct.

6. Break the code by removing the very last line of code, the single curly brace. (}) Press the Check syntax button again.
7. An alert opens as well as the Compiler Errors window. The description of the error is: 1084: Syntax error: expecting rightbrace before end of program.
8. Replace the right brace on the last line. Press Check syntax icon again to make sure the code is well formed again.
9. Open preferences. This can be done several ways.
   - From the menu at the top of the main workspace go to Edit > Preferences.
   - In the upper left of the Actions editor click on the context menu (the small icon of a black triangle and a stack of horizontal lines) directly below the close icon and select Preferences.
10. Choose the ActionScript category in the left side column of the Preferences window. Notice that many preferences can be set here including the font, size and color of the code.
11. Chose the Auto Format category in the left side column of the Preferences window.
12. Try different settings and notice how the sample code is reformatted. Pick a combination of formatting settings and click on the OK button to close the Preferences window.
13. In the Actions editor press the Auto Format icon. (It is on the right side of the Check syntax icon. It is a set of staggered horizontal lines.). The selected formatting options are applied to the code in the editor.

CHAPTER 2 – BASIC ELEMENTS OF ACTIONSCRIPT

Overview

This chapter introduces the basic elements of ActionScript; variables, functions conditional logic and loops.

Topics

- Variables
- Data types
- Comments
- Functions
- Conditional logic
- Loops

Variables

Related file: The following file contains the examples for this discussion. [class files] \basics\Example_variablesAndDataTyping.fla.

Variables are simply storage containers. They are places where we keep information. Variables can store numbers, words, references to movieClips, the number of the frame that the playback head is on and many other pieces of information. Variables are Tupperware for data. If a variable belongs to an object it is called a property.

The following example shows a variable being declared without assigning a value to it.

```
var myNumber:Number;
```

var is a keyword. Keywords are words that have special meanings and powers in ActionScript. The var keyword says that a new variable is being created.

myNumber is the name of the variable. Variable names can be almost anything but should always be descriptive. Variable names have very few restrictions on them. Variable naming conventions and restrictions were covered in the previous chapter.

:Number sets the type of data the variable will hold. This variable can only hold a number. Any attempt to store text or anything else in myNumber will cause an error.

The semicolon (;) indicates the end of a statement.

The equal sign (=), the assignment operator, is used to assign the variable a value.

```
myNumber = 3;
```

Variables can be created and assigned a value at the same time.

```
var myText:String = "Hello World";
```

In this example creating the variable and assigning it a value work the same as before, however both are done in the same statement. In this example the type of data being stored is different. Text is being stored instead of a number.

The data type for text is String (a string of letters). Because text is being assigned to the variable the text is placed in quotes. This tells Flash to take the text literally instead of trying to interpret them as variables or ActionScript keyword.

Unquoted words and letters will be interpreted by Flash to be ActionScript. Quoted words and letters will be taken literally and Flash will not try to interpret them as ActionScript. Because of this, quoted text is sometimes referred to as a string literal.

Comments

Commenting can be used to add notes to code or disable code from running. Both can be helpful during production and testing.

There are two ways to turn text in the script window into inactive notes. Two forward slashes (//) create a single line comment. A block comment begins with forward slash asterisk, is followed by the text for the comment, and closes with asterisk forward slash (/* some characters */).

```
// This line and the next two are comments.
// var someVar:Number = 9001;
// The next line is a statement.
var myVariable:String = "'sup";
/*
This is a block comment.
var variableOne:Number = 1;
var variableTwo:String = "shazbot";
*/
```

Data types

There are advantages to using variables that are limited to holding a specific type of data. These advantages include:

- Code hinting
- Clarity

When a variable is data typed code hints will appear (if available) when a dot (.) is entered after the variable name.

Data typing variables provides clarity during development because programmers know exactly the type of data they should have at any point. Strings are never confused with numbers. Dollars are never confused with dates. This can be very helpful when debugging.

Data typing can also prevent unexpected results when performing operations with variables. This will be demonstrated in an upcoming example.

Example – Variables and Data Typing

Example File

[class files] \basics\Example_variablesAndDataTyping.fla.

Overview

This example creates and assigns values to two variables.

The values stored in the variables are changed twice.

The first time values of the correct data types are assigned to the variables.

The second time values of the wrong data type are assigned to the variables.

Suggestions

1. Open and examine the file.
2. There are no objects on stage.
3. Select frame 1 of the actions layer.
4. Open the Actions editor.
5. Notice the actions in this script are a mix of comments and statements.
6. Run the file.
7. Notice that the Compiler Errors window opens.

In this example the attempts to assign the wrong data types to variables produce the following error messages:

1067: Implicit coercion of a value of type int to an unrelated type String.

1067: Implicit coercion of a value of type String to an unrelated type Number.

Implicit coercion means an attempt was made to change the data type of the value being assigned without specific (explicit) direction from the programmer.

int is a type of number.

The following are the numeric data types in ActionScript.

- **Number**
  Any numeric value, including values with or without a fraction.
- **Int**
  An integer (a whole number without a fraction).
- **uint**
  An "unsigned" integer, meaning a whole number that can't be negative.

Code – Variables and Data Typing

```
// Example of variables and data typing.

// Create variables and assign initial values.
var someString:String = "Life.";
var someNumber:Number = 0;

/*
The next two lines assign new values of
the correct type of data without error.
*/
someString = "The universe.";
someNumber = 42;

/*
These two lines attempt to assign new values
of the wrong type of data.
*/
someString = 23;
someNumber = "Everything.";
// These last two lines produce an error.
```

Functions

Related file: The following file contains the examples for this discussion. [class files]/basics/Example_traceTextAndStrings.fla.

Functions do things.

Variables hold information, functions hold instructions.

Flash applications are driven by functions. Functions can be thought of as macros; reusable blocks of code that are written once and reused as often as needed. Programmers can write their own functions or use the many functions built into ActionScript.

Functions and calls to functions are distinguished from variables by parentheses. Even if the parentheses are empty, all functions and function calls have parenthesis. The parentheses are there to pass and receive information. Information that is passed to functions is referred to as arguments or parameters.

Stop is a function often used with movieClips.

```
myMovieClip.stop();
```

The parentheses are empty because stop() does not need any extra information to work properly. stop() stops the playback head on whatever frame the playback head is on when the stop() command is issued.

Stop is a function that belongs to instances of the MovieClip class. When a function belongs to a class it is called a method.

Compare stop with another method; gotoAndStop.

```
myMovieClip.gotoAndStop(5);
```

The gotoAndStop method does require extra information. Here is where the parentheses are used. The number of the frame to stop on is passed to the function being called through the parentheses. The number of the frame can be referred to as an argument or a parameter.

The trace() function

A very useful function built into ActionScript is the trace function. Trace is a very handy tool to use during development.

The trace() function simply prints its parameters to the Output window. This only works during development when the file is launched from the Flash authoring tool. It does nothing at runtime when the .SWF is playing on the desktop or in a web page.

The trace() function can be used to get a look at the value of a variable at a specific point in the execution of the code. Traces can also be used to see if a certain point in the code is being reached.

The following example shows the use of a trace statement.

```
var textOne:String = "Foo";
var textTwo:String = "Bar";
trace( textOne + textTwo );
```

This example would print the word "FooBar" into the output window. The plus sign (+) is used as a concatenation operator to "add" the value of the two variables together. A space could be added between the two values by concatenating the string literal for a space in the middle of the expression.

```
trace( textOne + " " +  textTwo );
```

trace() is a global function. Global functions can be called from anywhere in an application.

Displaying text

Flash has a variety of text objects. They allow developers to write information to users (dynamic and input text). They also allow users to input information developers can use (input text).

Starting with Flash Player 10 a new type of text was introduced. The new text uses the Text Layout Framework (TLF). The TLF has many new features for working with text. Unfortunately CSS is not easily used with the new Text Layout Framework

The older, more compatible, CSS friendly Classic Text objects are used in this course.

Static text is not something that can be affected directly by ActionScript. Static text is a designer's tool, not a programmer's tool.

Text can be created by the text tool or the prebuilt text components can be used.

Different text objects can be configured and used in many different ways. They can be single line or multiline. They can be read only (dynamic) or the user can write into them (input). They can display (limited) HTML or plain text. They can have a scroll bars.

Just like MovieClips, text objects use instance names to identify them. After their name, the most commonly used property of text objects is the text property. The text property is used to read and write information to text objects. In addition there is an htmlText property that supports some basic HTML formatting to provide rich text display.

Displaying variables on the stage

If the value of a variable is a string it can easily be displayed in a text object on the stage. This does not work for text of the static type. It will work for all the other types of text objects.

Text objects have a variable to hold the text they display. The name of this variable is text. This variable is referred to as the text property of the text object.

The following is an example of assigning a string to the text property of a text object.

```
txtDisplay.text = "It works!";
```

Quotes

Typically strings are surrounded by double quotes. This is done by convention. Single quotes will also work.

If double quotes are needed within a string, surround the string with single quotes.

```
txtDisplay.text = 'He said; "Yo!"';
```

The escape character (\ ) can also be used to create a quote character regardless of the outer quotes used. An escaped single quote would be \' and an escaped double quote would be \".

```
txtDisplay.text = "He said; \"Yo!\"";
```

The this keyword

The this keyword is a variable. It is always a reference to the object that owns the piece of code the word this is used in. The keyword this always refers to the current object.

Here are some previous examples rewritten to use this.

```
var textOne:String = "Foo";
var textTwo:String = "Bar";

trace( this.textOne + this.textTwo );

this.txtDisplay.text = "It works!";
```

The use of this is almost always optional. It is only required in few very specific cases. Those cases are not encountered in this course.

Example – Trace, Text and String Concatenation

File

[class files]/basics/Example_traceTextAndStrings.fla.

Overview

This example creates and assigns values to three variables.

The variables are traced out two different ways. Two variables are concatenated and traced. All three variables are concatenated with spaces and assigned to a fourth variable.

The fourth variable is output in a trace statement and assigned to the text property of a dynamic textField.

Suggestion

1. Open and examine the file.
2. Notice that there is a dynamic textField on the stage with an instance name of txtDisplay.
3. Examine the actions in frame 1 of the actions layer.
4. Run the file.
5. Notice that the Output window opens.
6. The following output is displayed in the Output window: "'sup big dawg?".
7. The same text appears in the dynamic textField on the stage.

Code – Trace, Text and String Concatenation

```
// Create three string variables.
var firstWord:String = "'sup";
var secondWord:String = "big";
var thirdWord:String = "dawg?";

// Output the value of two variables.
trace(secondWord + thirdWord);

// Concatenate the 3 variables into 1 easy to use
variable.
// Add spaces between the words.
var greeting:String = firstWord + " " + secondWord + "
" + thirdWord;

// Output the variable using trace().
trace(greeting);

// Write the variable to a text object on the stage.
txtDisplay.text = greeting;
```

Casting a data type

Related file: The following file contains the examples for this discussion. [class files]/basics/Example_casting.fla.

There are times when it is necessary, and possible, to change data from one data type to another. Changing a data type from one type to another is called casting. Not all data types can be cast as another type.

One case where casting is necessary is when trying to assign a number to the text property of a text object.

The following example will produce a compiler error.

```
txtDisplay.text = 33;
```

1067: Implicit coercion of a value of type int to an unrelated type String.

The following example shows how numbers can be converted to a string.

```
txtDisplay.text = String(33);
```

This will convert the number 33 to a string and assign it to the text object without error.

Unexpected results

Operations on mixed data types can sometimes cause unexpected results from mathematical operations.

Mixing strings and numbers when using the + operator is a common cause of unexpected results. If both values are numeric addition occurs. If either value is a string then concatenation occurs.

The following example casts a string as a number:

```
var numberAsString:String = "1";
var myNumber:Number = Number(numberAsString);
```

Putting quotes around the number ("1") represents it as text, not a number. The addition operator will not perform mathematical operations on the text represented by the variable numberAsString. Instead concatenation will occur.

The string represented by numberAsString can be transformed to a number by the expression: Number(numberAsString). This allows mathematical operations to work properly on the variable.

Example – Casting

Example File

[class files]/basics/Example_casting.fla.

Overview

This example creates two variables holding the value 1. The myNumber variable holds 1 as a number. The myString variable holds 1 as a string.

Operations are then performed on the variables using the + operator.

The variables are also applied to the text property of a text object.

Suggestions

1. Open and examine the file.
2. Notice that there is a dynamic text field on the stage with an instance name of txtDisplay. It is used later in this example.
3. Examine the actions in frame 1 of the actions layer.
4. Run the file.
5. The Output window opens.
6. Examine the output.
7. Any + operation involving a string resulted in concatenation.
8. Only + operations on two numbers produced mathematical addition.
9. Turn the comment // txtDisplay.text = myNumber; into a line of code by removing the two slashes at the beginning of the line.
10. Run the file and notice the data type error.
11. Turn txtDisplay.text = myNumber; back into a comment by placing two slashes back at the start of the line.
12. Turn the comment: txtDisplay.text = String(myNumber); into a line of code by removing the two slashes at the beginning of that line.
13. Run the file and notice that the value of myNumber displays in the textField on the stage without error.

Code – Casting

```
// Set a variable to the number 1.
var myNumber:Number = 1;
// Set a variable to the string 1.
var myString:String = "1";

// Try doing some addition:
// Correct result.
trace("1 + 1 =");
trace(myNumber + myNumber);
// Correct result.
trace('"1" + "1" =');
trace(myString + myString);
// Unexpected result.
trace('1 + "1" =');
trace(myNumber + myString);
// Cast the string as a number.
trace('1 + Number("1") =');
trace(myNumber + Number(myString));

// Numbers assigned to a text property don't work.
// txtDisplay.text = myNumber;

// Casting the number to a string works.
// txtDisplay.text = String(myNumber);
```

Variables in timelines

Related file: No file. This short discussion leads right into an exercise.

So far, all of the examples have used ActionScript in the first frame of one frame movies. In many applications variables will be used in longer timelines. Variables may be used in the main time line or inside a movieClip's timeline.

Variables do not exist just in the frame in which they are created. Once created, variables exist throughout the timeline of the object they were created in. This means that variables holding user names, number of tries, answers, scores etc. are available in any frame in the timeline of the object that they are created in.

ActionScript must be declared in a keyframe. An actions layer may hold more than one keyframe and each keyframe can have its own ActionScript statements. This provides a simple way to execute ActionScript on specific frames at specific times in a movie.

A variable can be used to track how many times a movie has played in a loop. This will be the subject of the next exercise.

In a later exercise this variable will be used with conditional logic to keep a movie from looping endlessly.

Compound Operators

Programmers have several operations that are used a lot. They have developed shortcuts for these operations called compound operators.

Here are some of the most common operations and their shortcut equivalents.

```
z = z + 1;
++z;

z = z - 1;
--z;

z = z + 10;
z += 10;
```

```
z = z - 10;
z -= 10;

z = z * 10;
z *= 10;

z = z / 10;
z /= 10;
```

Try it – Timeline Variables

Challenge

Create a variable that tracks how many times a movie has played in a loop. Use a trace statement at the end of the timeline to display the variable every time it is incremented. In the last exercise of this chapter the variable will be used to keep the movie from looping continuously.

There are suggestions for solving the challenge on this page. The following page offers a solution. A starter file has been provided.

Starter file

[class files]/basics/Begin_variablesInTimelines.fla.

The starter file has an actions layer. There are 25 frames in the actions layer. There are keyframes in the action's layer first and last frame with a few helpful comments.

Suggestion

1. Open, examine and run the file. The movie plays continuously and shows photos of different cars.
2. In the first frame create a variable to count how many times the movie has played and give it an initial value of 0.
3. In the last frame add 1 to the value of the counting variable every time the playback head reaches the last frame.
4. Trace out the value of the counting variable in the last frame after it is increased by 1.
5. Run the file and observe the output. Notice the variable does not increase past 1. Why? The playback head returns to frame 1 and recreates the counter variable.
6. Do not allow the playback head to loop naturally back to frame 1. This resets the variable back to its initial value.
7. Send the playback head to frame 2 after increasing the counter. Use frame labels for navigation instead of frame numbers.

Solution – Timeline Variables

Solution file

[class files]/basics/Solution_ variablesInTimelines.fla.

This file provides one possible solution for the challenge.

In frame 1

```
// Create a variable to hold number of times movie
played.
var counter:Number = 0;
```

In the last frame

```
// Add 1 to the value stored in counter.
// counter = counter + 1;
counter++

// Display the value stored in counter.
trace(counter);

// Go back to the second frame instead of frame 1.
// Going back to frame 1 would reset the counter to 0.
gotoAndPlay("startLoop");
```

Conditional logic

Related file: The following file contains the examples for this discussion. [class files]/basics/Example_ifStatements.fla.

Variables store information. Functions get things done.

Conditional logic makes decisions.

Conditional logic consists of tests which determine if some condition is true. Based on the result of the tests a programmer can take any action they need to.

Conditional logic can be very simple, having only one test and one result. Conditional logic can also be quite complex performing many tests and having more tests nested inside.

ActionScript provides two types of conditional logic; if statements and case statements. This chapter examines if statements.

If statements

The structure of an if statement is easy to understand. A condition is tested and if the condition is true the actions in the body of the if statement are executed.

Opening and closing curly braces ({ }) are used to define the blocks of code associated with the conditions.

```
if (The statement here is true.)
{
  Do this.
}
```

If statements contain one or more evaluations and have the following general form:

```
if ( predicate )   // If this is true.
{
   --consequent--;  // Do this.
}
else  // If the predicate is false.
{
   --alternative--;  // Do this.
}
```

If the first evaluation, called the predicate, is true the first block of code, called the consequent clause, runs. The predicate can be a complex expression but it is common to simply test the value of a variable or property.

Once any predicate evaluates as true the if statement stops processing.

When checking to see if two things are equal the equal sign (=) is not used. The equal sign by itself is the assignment operator and is used to assign values. When testing for equality the equality operator, two equal signs (==), are used.

A simple if statement may only have a single predicate. In this example if the predicate evaluates to false nothing happens.

```
var someValue:String = "fun";

if ( someValue == "fun" )
{
   trace("We like " + someValue);
}
```

Else clauses

An else clause can be added to an if statement. If the predicate does not evaluates to true an alternative block of code runs.

```
var anotherValue:String = "boring";

if (anotherValue == "fun" )
{
   trace("We like " + anotherValue);
}
else
{
   trace("We don't like " + anotherValue);
}
```

The example above produces an output of: “We don’t like boring.”

Else clauses are always optional.

Else if clauses

Else if clauses allow for multiple tests to be run in the same if statement. Else if clauses follow the initial if clause. When any clause tests true the if statement stops testing conditions.

The following example tests a variable to determine the season.

```
var season:String = "fall";

if ( season == "spring" )
{
   trace("Flowers bloom in spring.");
}
else if ( season == "summer" )
{
   trace("Summer is hot.");
}
else if ( season == "fall" )
{
   trace("Leaves turn colors in the fall.");
}
else if ( season == "winter" )
{
   trace("It is cold in the winter.");
}
```

An else clause could be added at the end of this example if an action was required if none of the other conditions evaluated as true.

When one variable is the subject of several tests developers sometimes prefer to write the logic in the form of a switch statement. Switch statements are covered in the next class. An if statement with else if clauses can provide the same functionality as a switch statement.

The NOT (!) operator

The NOT operator (!) reverses the logic of a test. It can be used by itself or with other logical operators. Instead of testing to see if two values are equal (==) the two values can be tested to see that they are not equal (!=).

The NOT operator can be very useful by itself. It can be used to see if a variable already exists. This can prevent unwanted re-initialization of variables.

The following is an example of using the NOT operator to initialize a variable only once.

```
if(! myVar)
{
     var myVar:Number = 0;
}
```

This can be read as: "If myVar does not exist then initialize my var. If myVar does exist then do nothing".

Logical operators

Logical operators can be used to create expressions for evaluation.

The following are some of the logical operators.

==	Is equal to
!=	Is NOT equal to
>	Greater than
<	Less than
<=	Less than or equal to
>=	Greater than or equal to

Compound conditional expressions

Compound conditional operators allow for more than one test to be conducted in a predicate. These conditional operators allow the creation of compound logical expressions. These conditional operators are the logical AND operator (&&) and the logical OR operator (| |).

The OR operator allows either condition to be true. The AND operator requires both conditions to be true.

The following expression is pseudo code (not real ActionScript) but illustrates the use of the AND operator.

```
if (today > Friday && today < Monday)
{
  // It's the weekend! :)
}
```

The OR operator allows either expressions to be true. This allows us to restate the previous example.

```
if (today == Saturday || today == Sunday)
{
  // It's the weekend! Happy, happy, joy, joy!
}
```

Example – If statements

Example file

[class files]/basics/Example_ifStatements.fla.

Overview

The example file demonstrates several variations of if statements.

Suggestions

1. Open and examine the file.
2. Notice that there is nothing on stage. All output is from trace statements.
3. Examine the actions in frame 1 of the actions layer.
4. Run the file.
5. Observe the output.
6. Change the code, either the variables or the conditions, to produce different output.

Code - If statements

```
// A simple if statement.
var someValue:String = "fun";
if (someValue == "fun" )
{
   trace("We like " + someValue + ".");
}

// If with an else clause.
var anotherValue:String = "boring";
if (anotherValue == "fun" )
{
   trace("We like " + anotherValue + ".");
}
else
{
   trace("We don't like " + anotherValue + ".");
}

// If with else if clauses.
var season:String = "fall";
if ( season == "spring" )
{
   trace("Flowers bloom in spring.");
}
else if ( season == "summer" )
{
   trace("Summer is hot.");
}
else if ( season == "fall" )
{
   trace("Leaves turn colors in the fall.");
}
else if ( season == "winter" )
{
   trace("It is cold in the winter.");
}
```

Code continues on the next page...

Code – If statements (continued)

```
// If with a logical OR.
var theDayOfTheWeek:String = "Monday";
if (theDayOfTheWeek == "Saturday" || theDayOfTheWeek
== "Sunday")
{
   trace("Weekends Rock!!!");
}
else
{
   trace("It's a workday.");
}
```

Controlling movie playback

Related file: No file. This short discussion leads right into an exercise.

If statements can be used to change how a movie runs based on data from the player or variables created by a user.

A user could be blocked from parts of the movie if they are not logged in. They could be taken to different parts of the movie depending on a selection they made earlier in the movie. Different content could be loaded based on the value of variables set by user choices. A user's score could control game play.

Another use of conditional logic is to keep a movie from looping endlessly. This is often a requirement for banner ads. The elements of ActionScript that have been presented in this chapter provide enough tools to accomplish this task.

Loops

Loops allow for the easy automation of repetitive actions. There are a number of different types of loops available in ActionScript.

The advanced course on ActionScript covers loops in detail.

The next chapter in this course will use a special loop to prevent the same random number from being created twice in a row.

Try it – Controlling playback

Challenge

Stop a movie from looping after it has played three times. Allow the movie to loop back into frame 1.

There is a suggestion for solving the challenge on this page. The following page offers a solution. A starter file has been provided.

Starter file

[class files]/basics/Begin_controllingPlayback.fla.

The starter file is a timeline driven slide show intended as a banner ad. It continues the work done in the variables in timeline exercise.

Suggestions

1. Open and examine the starter file.
   Notice that the labels layer has been removed. It will not be needed.
2. In the first frame use conditional logic to keep the variable from being reset when the movie loops back to frame 1.
3. Create an if statement in the last frame of the actions layer:
4. Test the value of the counter after it has been increased.
5. Stop the movie if the movie has played three times.
6. Allow the move to loop naturally back to frame 1 if the movie has not played three times.
7. Run the file and test your work.

Solution – Controlling playback

Solution file

[class files]/basics/Solution_controllingPlayback.fla

This file provides a possible solution for the challenge.

Frame 1 of the actions layer

A variable to hold the number of times the movie has played is created. It is kept from being reinitialized when the movie loops by the if statement.

```
if(! counter)
{
   var counter:Number = 0;
}
```

Last frame of the actions layer

The value of the counter is increased by one. If the value of counter is 3 the movie stops. If the value of counter is not 3 the movie continues to play.

```
// counter = counter +1;
++counter;
if ( counter == 3 )
{
   stop();
}
```

CHAPTER 3 – OOP IN TEN WORDS OR LESS

Overview

This chapter tells you all you really ever need to know about object oriented programming.

Topics

- Objects
- Properties
- Methods
- Classes

Object oriented programming is just a way of looking at programming problems and organizing programming solutions. An object is just a thing that holds information and can do things.

Variables store information. When a variable belongs to an object it is called a property.

Functions do things. When a function belongs to an object it is called a method.

An object is simply a collection of methods and/or properties related to some purpose.

A movieClip is a familiar example of an object. MovieClips have properties that hold information about them. A movieClip's name is an example of a property. A movieClip can do things such as stop and play. Those are examples of some of a movieClip's methods.

Nine words

- Objects are nouns.
- Properties are adjectives.
- Methods are verbs.

Classes

A class is simply a collection of methods and properties. A class file defines the variables and functions that belong to an object. A class file is the model, the blueprint, for a specific type of object.

That is really all there is to it. When a developer wants to get something done they ask, "Is there a class to do what I want? What are its properties and methods?" Good documentation and examples are all a developer needs to work with new classes if they are familiar with the rest of the development environment.

That was it. All you need to know about object oriented programming is on the other side of this page.

CHAPTER 4 – EVENTS AND EVENT HANDLING

Overview

Responding to events from users and events created by objects is a common task for developers.

In this chapter event handling will be used to create a versatile, interactive slide show. Functionality for the slide show includes allowing the user to jump to a random frame and to navigate back and forth through the slides.

Timing will be driven by a timer instead of adding and removing frames between slides. This will make the slide show's timing easy to change.

Topics

- Events
- Event handlers/listeners
- The event object
- Event names and constants
- The Math class
- Random numbers
- Rounding numbers
- Do while loops
- MovieClip timeline properties
- The Timer class

Events

Related file: The following file contains the examples for this discussion. [class files]/eventHandling/Example_eventsAndMath.fla.

Everything in Flash is event driven. Nothing just happens. Everything happens in response to some event.

Some events are generated by Flash. A simple thing like the frame rate broadcasts enterFrame events. Retrieving data may generate a result event.

Other events may be generated by users. Users may click on, roll over or roll out of an object.

Event listeners

Events are handled by assigning functions to respond to them. These functions are called listeners, event handlers or just handlers. Event handlers are assigned using the addEventListener() method.

The following generic example assigns an event handler to an event from someObject.

```
// Assign an event handler.
someObject.addEventListener("anEvent", eventHandler);
```

This example can be read as; when someObject generates anEvent run the eventHandler function.

Different objects will create specific events depending on what type of object they are.

Event handlers have the following general form.

```
// Event handler function.
function eventHandler(event:Event):void
{
  // Respond to the event here;
}
```

An event handler is much like a normal function. It has one unique feature, a variable (called an argument or parameter) that is automatically passed to the parenthesis of the function. That argument is automatically passed to the function simply because the function has been assigned as the handler for an event.

The name of the argument is up to the user. It is the name on the left of the colon. It can be called anything. In practice it is often called event, e or evt.

The data type, the name to the right of the colon, can be simply Event unless a more specific event type is needed. Different Event objects may contain special properties related to their specific event type.

The event argument can be used as a variable inside the handler. The event object holds lots of useful information about the event. The event object will be discussed in greater detail in the next chapter where it will be used to simplify event handling.

The :void at the end of the first line of the handler indicates that all the work is being done inside the handler. No information is being returned to the caller of the function.

The listeners can be assigned and the handlers declared in any order. Some developers write the handlers first and then assign the listeners at the bottom of the page. It is more common to assign the listeners at the top of the file. The listeners are usually assigned after any variables are declared and before the functions are created.

Event names

There are two very different ways to write event names. One way is to refer to the event as a simple string such as "click" or "enterFrame". This is a simple and common practice. There are also constant representations of the event names such as MouseEvent.CLICK or Event.ENTER_FRAME. Using the constant representation of the event name is considered the best practice.

Event constants

Constants are simply variables whose values are assigned one time and then cannot be changed. Their value stays constant throughout the application. They are read only variables.

The value PI from the Math class is a good example of a constant. Even if we were tempted to try to round PI off to 3 the expression Math.PI = 3 will throw an error.

By convention constants are written in all caps. Constants use underscores instead of intra-capitalization to separate words. For example the string representation of the event would be "mouseOver" while the constant representation would be MouseEvent.MOUSE_OVER.

Event constants and errors

Using constants for events provides better feedback about spelling mistakes. This helps with troubleshooting and debugging. Using the constants will also provide code hints while typing the code.

Consider the following example. The event name, click, has been misspelled with an extra i in both the constant and the string representation of the event.

```
stage.addEventListener(MouseEvent.CLIiCK, handler1);

stage.addEventListener("cliick", handler1);

function handler1 (event:Event)
{
   trace( "handler1 called" );
}
```

When the file is run the misspelling of the string will produce no error messages. Even worse, the button will fail to operate without any indication why.

The misspelling of the constant will give the following error as soon as the file is launched:

```
1119: Access of possibly undefined property CLIiCK
through a reference with static type Class.
```

Spelling errors are often reported as an "undefined property" error.

The Math class

The Math class has useful methods for creating random numbers and rounding numbers off. This can be useful for game development or displaying random images in a slide show.

The Math class and a loop will be used in the slide show that will be built in this chapter. Together, they will generate a random frame number to show a random slide.

The Math class is not used to create instances, it is used directly. Methods and properties of the Math class are called directly against the Math class.

```
Math.PI;

Math.random();
```

Math.random

Math.random() generates a random number from 0 to less than one. To make this random number more useful it is multiplied by a number.

This following expression creates fractional numbers with a range from greater than 0 and less than 3.

```
Math.random() * 3;
```

The Math class has 3 ways of rounding off numbers. Math.floor() rounds down. Math.ceil() rounds up. Math.round() rounds to the nearest number.

Using Math.ceil in following expression creates a random whole number from 1 and 10, inclusive.

```
Math.ceil( Math.random() * 10 );
```

Generating a different random number every time

A special type of loop can be used to prevent the same random number from being generated twice. A do while loop is perfect for this purpose.

A do while loop delays evaluating the condition for the loop until after the body of the loop. This means that a do while loop always runs at least once. It continues to run until the condition in the while clause is false. The following is an example of the general form of a do while loop.

```
do
{
   // Actions to be performed.
} while ( This expression is true.);
```

The next example shows a do while loop used in a handler to prevent the same number from being generated twice.

```
// Create two variables. Do not assign values to them.
var newNumber:Number;
var oldNumber:Number;

button.addEventListener(MouseEvent.CLICK,
                        buttonHandler);

function buttonHandler(event:Event)
{
   // The do while loop will run until...
   // ...the condition in the while clause is false.
   do
   {
        newNumber = Math.ceil(Math.random() * 3);
   } while (newNumber == oldNumber);

   // Record the number that was just generated.
   // Used the next time the do while loop runs to
   // prevent same number from being generated twice.
   oldNumber = newNumber;

   // Use the new number.
   trace(newNumber);
}
```

Example – Event handling and the Math class

Example file

[class files]/eventHandling/Example_eventsAndMath.fla.

Overview

The example file demonstrates event handling and random number generation. There are three buttons, labels for the buttons and a dynamic text field on the stage.

Suggestions

1. Open, examine and run the file. Click on each of the buttons.
2. Notice that all the buttons write information to the stage.
3. Examine the actions in frame 1.
    a. Button1's handler is assigned using the string representation of the event.
    b. Button2's handler is assigned using the event constant. button2's handler generates a decimal and a whole random number
    c. Button3's handler generates a decimal and a whole random number. The handler also uses the newline character (\n) to break its output into two lines. Button3's handler generates a random rounded whole number. A do while loop is used to prevent generating the same random number two times in a row.
4. Misspell the click event in the line:
   button1.addEventListener("click", button1Handler);
5. Run the file and click button1.
    a. It fails silently with no error messages.
    b. Correct the spelling.
6. Misspell CLICK in MouseEvent.CLICK in the line:
   button2.addEventListener(MouseEvent.CLICK, button2Handler);
7. Run the file.

a. Notice that an error message immediately appears.

b. Correct the spelling.

8. Run the file and click on button 2 repeatedly. Notice that:
   a. The decimal number is different every time.
   b. Sometimes the new rounded number is the same as the previous rounded number. This could cause an application to appear to act as if nothing happened when the button was clicked.
9. Run the file and click on button 3 repeatedly. Notice that the same number never appears twice in a row.

Code – Event handling and the Math class

```
// button1 ------------------------------------------
button1.addEventListener("click", button1Handler);

function button1Handler(event:Event)
{
   txtDisplay.text = "button1Handler called";
}

// button2 ------------------------------------------
button2.addEventListener(MouseEvent.CLICK,
button2Handler);

function button2Handler(event:Event)
{
   var randomNumber:Number = Math.random() * 3;
   txtDisplay.text = "Without rounding:  " +
   randomNumber +
   "\n" + "With Math.round(): " +
   Math.round(randomNumber);
}
```

Code continues on next page...

Code – Event handling and the Math class (continued)

```
// button3 -------------------------------------------
var newNumber:Number;
var oldNumber:Number;
button3.addEventListener(MouseEvent.CLICK,
button3Handler);

function button3Handler(event:Event)
{
   // This do while loop will run until...
   // ...the condition in the while clause is false.
   do
   {
        newNumber = Math.ceil(Math.random() * 3);
   } while (newNumber == oldNumber);

   // Record the number that was just generated.
   // It will be used the next time
      the do while loop runs...
   // ...to prevent the same number
   // ...from being generated twice.
   oldNumber = newNumber;

   // Use the new number for something.
   txtDisplay.text = String(newNumber);
}
```

MovieClip timeline properties and methods

Related file: No file. This short discussion leads right into an exercise.

The MovieClip class has several methods and properties useful for navigation.

The currentFrame and totalFrames properties

The MovieClip class has two properties that are very useful when navigating timelines. The two properties are currentFrame and totalFrames.

Both properties are read only. They cannot be changed via ActionScript.

The currentFrame property gives the number of the frame that the playback head is on. The currentFrame property can be read. It cannot be assigned a value to cause the movie to go to that frame.

totalFrames is a movieClip property that gives the number of frames in a timeline. This can be used to create an expression that provides a random number from 1 to the last frame of the movie. This will permit the expression to work in any timeline without having to edit the expression to update the timeline's length.

The following expression can be used with navigation methods such as gotoAndStop() to randomly jump to any frame in a timeline of any length.

```
Math.ceil(Math.random() * totalFrames);
```

Notice that the random number is rounded up using Math.ceil(). This creates numbers between 1 and the total number of frames.

The nextFrame() and prevFrame() methods

These two methods are simple and intuitive. They move the playback head one frame forward or backward.

Going to a different random frame every time

Using MovieClip timeline properties simplifies generating a different frame number every time. Since movieClip properties are used, one less variable is needed. The one user variable that is needed can be declared right in the handler.

The following example modifies the previous do while example to generate a random frame number instead of just a random number.

```
button.addEventListener(MouseEvent.CLICK,
clickHandler);

function clickHandler(event:Event)
{
   // Declare a variable to hold the random number.
   var randomFrame:Number;
   do
   {
        // Generate a number from 1 to
           the last frame in the timeline.
        randomFrame =
            Math.ceil(Math.random() * totalFrames);
   } while (randomFrame == currentFrame);

   gotoAndStop(randomFrame);
}
```

Declaring variables inside a function

Notice that the randomFrame variable is declared inside the function. If a variable is only used inside the function the best practice is to declare that variable inside the function. This creates a temporary variable that exists only while the function is being called. After the function is done running the variable disappear from memory. This saves on memory.

Try it – Jump to a random frame

Challenge

Write a handler that jumps to a random frame each time the user clicks on a button.

There is a suggestion for solving the challenge on this page. Starter files have been provided with two different levels of challenge.

Starter files

Two different starting files are provided. Each one offers a different level of challenge. Choose the file with the level of challenge that is the most comfortable for you.

> **Standard** - This file has just a few helpful comments.
> [class files]/eventHandling/Begin_randomFrame.fla.
>
> **Fill in the blanks** - The skeleton of the code is provided. Three question marks (???) have been placed everywhere more information is needed.
> [class files]/ eventHandling/Begin_randomFrame_Comments.fla.

The starter file is an image gallery. There is one image in each frame of the main timeline. A stop action in frame 1 keeps the movie from playing automatically. There is a button on the stage named btnRandom.

Suggestions

1. Assign a listener to btnRandom to respond to mouse clicks.
2. Write the handler function.
3. Inside the handler generate a random frame number.
    - Use the number of frames in the movie as the multiplier.
    - Use the totalFrames variable instead of the literal number of frames.
    - Round the random number up to a whole number.
    - Use a do while loop to keep from going to the same frame twice in a row.
4. Use the random number to make the movie go to that frame number and stop.

Solution – Jump to a random frame.

File: [class files]/eventHandling/Solution_randomFrame.fla

Here is one possible solution to the challenge.

```
// Hold the movie here on frame one.
stop();

// Assign listener------------------------
btnRandom.addEventListener(MouseEvent.CLICK,
                           gotoRandomFrame);

// Event handler--------------------------
// Write the handler.
function gotoRandomFrame(event:Event):void
{
   // Declare a variable to hold the random frame
number.
   var randomFrame:Number;
   // Use a do while loop to prevent generating the...
   // ...same random number twice in a row.
   do
   {
        // Generate a number from 1 to the last...
        // ...frame in the timeline.
        randomFrame =
        Math.ceil(Math.random() * totalFrames);
        // Continue the do while loop while...
        // ...the random frame is the current frame.
   } while (randomFrame == currentFrame);
    // Go to the random frame and stop.
   gotoAndStop(randomFrame);
}
```

Navigating through timelines

Related file: No file. This short discussion leads right into an exercise.

Buttons, event handlers and movieClip properties can be used to allow the user to navigate through the frames of a movie. The previous example navigated to a random frame. It is also possible to create navigation that moves linearly through a movie both forward and backward.

A decision has to be made on what to do when the playback head reaches either end of the timeline. The playback head could just stop at the last frame (when going forward) or the first frame (when going backward).

A more elegant solution, especially for a slide show, is to have the playback head go "around the corner". Going forward, after the playback head gets to the last frame it starts back over on frame 1. Going backward, after the playback head gets to the first frame it goes to the last frame.

Two handlers are needed, one for the "next" button and another for the "back" button. Each handler will have an if statement and an else clause in its body.

In the forward handler an if statement will see if the current frame is equal to the last frame of the movie. If it is, the movie will jump to frame 1 of the movie. Otherwise it will go to the next frame.

In the back handler an if statement will see if the movie is on the first frame. If it is, the movie will jump to the last frame of the movie. Otherwise it will go to the previous frame.

Feedback to the user

There may be times when a developer wants to provide the user with feedback about which frame they are on. The current frame number can be written into a text object on the stage.

If an attempt is made to write either the currentFrame or totalFrames property into the text property of a text field an implicit coercion error will be thrown.

The currentFrame or totalFrames properties should be cast to strings before assigning to a text property. Concatenation with a string would also cast the properties as strings.

```
text1.text = String(currentFrame);
text2.text = "Frame #" + currentFrame);
```

Sample logic for slide show navigation

```
// Logic in next handler.
   // Use an if statement to see if the...
   // ...current frame is the last frame.
   if (currentFrame == totalFrames)
   {
        gotoAndStop( 1 );
   }
   else
   {
        // Go to the next frame.
        nextFrame();
   }



// Logic in back handler.
   // Use an if statement to see if...
   // ...the current frame is frame 1.
   if (currentFrame == 1)
   {
        // If on frame 1 go to last frame.
        gotoAndStop( totalFrames );
   }
   else //Otherwise.
   {
        // Go to the previous frame.
        prevFrame();
   }
```

Try it – Navigating through a timeline

Challenge

Write two handlers that move the playback head forward and backward through a timeline. When the playback head reaches one end of the timeline have it jump to the other end. Every time the frame changes show the user the frame they are on.

There is a suggestion for solving the challenge on this page. The following page offers a Solution. Starter files have been provided with two different levels of challenge.

Starter Files

Two different starting files are provided. Each one offers a different level of challenge. Choose the level that is the most comfortable for you. The files with the comments and the skeleton of the code can be examined to provide you with additional hints to help you solve the challenge.

> **Challenging** - This file has the minimum amount of help.
> [class files]/ eventHandling/Begin_navigation.fla.
>
> **Fill in the blanks** - The skeleton of the code is provided. Three question marks (???) have been placed everywhere more information is needed. The missing information can be found in the examples in this chapter.
> [class files]/ eventHandling/Begin_navigation_FillInTheBlanks.fla.

About the starter files

The starter files use the image gallery from the random navigation example. The code and button for the random navigation are still in the starter files.

Two buttons have been added with the instance names btnNext and btnBack.

A text field has been added to the stage with the instance name txtFeedback.

Suggestions

1. Write the initial display of the frame number to txtFeedback.
2. Assign listeners to btnNext and btnBack.

3. Write the handlers for btnNext and btnBack.
4. In the next handler:
   - Use an if statement to test if the current frame is equal to the last frame of the movie.
   - If it is the last frame have the movie jump to frame 1.
   - Otherwise go to the next frame.
5. In the back handler (hint - copy and modify forward handler):
   - Use an if statement to test if the current frame is the first frame of the movie.
   - If it is the first frame have the movie jump to the last frame.
   - Otherwise have the movie go to the previous frame.
6. In both the btnNext and btnBack handlers update txtFeedback. Use the currentFrame property as the value to show in txtFeedback. Cast currentFrame as a string to prevent errors.
7. Update txtFeedback in the gotoRandomFrame handler.

Solution – Navigating through a timeline

File: [class files]/eventHandling/Solution_Navigation.fla.

Here is one possible solution to the challenge.

```
// Hold the movie here on frame one.
stop();

// Initialize the user feedback.
txtFeedback.text = String(currentFrame);

// Assign handlers-------------------------
// Add listeners for the next and back buttons.
btnNext.addEventListener(MouseEvent.CLICK, doNext);
btnBack.addEventListener(MouseEvent.CLICK, doBack);

random_btn.addEventListener(MouseEvent.CLICK,
                             gotoRandomFrame);

// Write the handlers for the next and back buttons.
// Next handler.
function doNext(event:Event):void
{
   // Use an if statement to see if the...
   // ...current frame is the last frame.
   if (currentFrame == totalFrames)
   {
        // If on last frame go to frame 1.
        gotoAndStop( 1 );
   }
   else
   {
        // Go to the next frame.
        nextFrame();
   }
   // Update the user feedback.
   txtFeedback.text = String(currentFrame);

}
```

The solution continues on the next page...

Solution – Navigating through a timeline (continued)

```
// Back handler.
function doBack(event:Event):void
{
   // Use an if statement to see if...
   // ...the current frame is frame 1.
   if (currentFrame == 1)
   {
        // If on frame 1 go to last frame.
        gotoAndStop( totalFrames );
   }
   else //Otherwise.
   {
        // Go to the previous frame.
        prevFrame();
   }
   // Update the user feedback.
   txtFeedback.text = String(currentFrame);
}

function gotoRandomFrame(event:Event):void
{
   // Declare a variable to hold the random frame
number.
   var randomFrame:Number;
   // Use a do while loop to prevent generating the...
   // ...same random number twice in a row.
   do
   {
        // Generate a number from 1 to
           the last frame in the timeline.
        randomFrame =
        Math.round(Math.random() * totalFrames);
        // Continue the do while loop while...
        // ...the random frame is the current frame.
   } while (randomFrame == currentFrame);
    // Go to the random frame and stop.
   gotoAndStop(randomFrame);
   txtFeedback.text = String(currentFrame);
}
```

Moving through a timeline with a timer

Related file: No file. This short discussion leads right into an exercise.

Animators often control slide show timing by adding or removing frames between images in a timeline. While this is simple and effective, changes to the movie's timing can be tedious and time consuming. Another issue with frame based timing occurs when such a movie is loaded into another movie. The loaded movie is run at the frame rate of the movie it is loaded into. This could cause the loaded movie to play too fast or too slow.

ActionScript has a timer object that can be used for many things including driving the playback head. A timer object generates timer events at a specific interval and for a specific amount of repetitions.

The following example shows the general form of the expression used to create timer objects.

```
var timer:Timer = new Timer(delay, repeatCount);
```

The delay argument specifies the time between calls to the timer handler in milliseconds (1,000ths of a second). The repeatCount argument specifies how many times the timer should run. A value of 0 for the repeatCount argument will cause the timer to run indefinitely.

Timers must be started before they begin generating events. They can be stopped and restarted.

The following example creates a timer, assigns a handler and starts the timer.

```
var timer:Timer = new Timer(4000, 0);
timer.start();

timer.addEventListener(TimerEvent.TIMER,
timerHandler);

function timerHandler(event:TimerEvent):void
{
   //Do things here.
}
```

Problems can occur when the playback head reenters the frame that creates and starts the timer. This can be prevented by wrapping the creation and initial starting of the timer in an if statement as was done with the counter variable in the previous chapter. The if statement will only create and start the timer if the timer does not exist.

Try it – Using a timer

Challenge

Use a timer to play the frames in a movie sequentially. Have the sequence start again from frame 1 when it reaches the end of the movie.

There is a suggestion for solving the challenge on this page. The following page offers a Solution. Starter files have been provided with three levels of challenge.

Starter File

[class files]/introduction/Begin_timer.fla.

The starter file is the image gallery used for the slide show in the other examples in this chapter.

The next handler is already written. It can be used as the timer handler.

The timer will need to be stopped and restarted when the user navigates the slide show. If this is not done the playback will appear erratic.

Suggestions

1. Create a timer.
   - Set the delay for a few seconds.
   - Choose a repeat count or have the timer run infinitely.
   - Start the timer.
2. Write the timer handler. The timer handler can call the doNext handler since it needs to do the same thing as a user clicking the next button.
3. Test and let it run through a few cycles of all the slides. Watch the timing of the playback closely.
4. Test again and navigate using the random, next and back buttons. Be sure to go to frame 1 several times. Watch the timing of the playback closely.
5. The timing gets thrown off the more times the playback head reenters frame 1. This is caused be recreating the timer every time the playback head enters frame 1.

6. Use an if statement and the NOT operator to keep the timer from being recreated and restarted in frame 1.
7. Test again. Automatic playback should be fine. Using the navigation controls still produces choppy playback. The reason is that the timer is running as the user changes the frame. It may have 2 seconds left before it automatically changes the frame again. Or the timer may only have 2 milliseconds left. The timer should be reset every time the user navigates.
8. Stop and restart the timer every time the user navigates to the next or previous frame.
9. Test again. The playback should be smooth.

Solution – Using a timer

File: [class files]/eventHandling/Solution_timer.fla.

This is one solution to the challenge. Only the new code is in bold. The gotoRandomFrame handler has not changed from the last example and is omitted.

```
// Hold the movie here on frame one.
stop();

// Initialization--------------------------

// Initialize the timer.
// Use an if statement to initialize...
// ...the timer only once.
if (!timer)
{
   // Create the timer.
   var timer:Timer = new Timer(4000, 0);
   // Start the timer.
   timer.start();
}

txtFeedback.text = String(currentFrame);


// Assign handlers------------------------

// Assign the timer handler.
timer.addEventListener(TimerEvent.TIMER, doNext);

// Button handlers.
btnNext.addEventListener(MouseEvent.CLICK, doNext);
btnBack.addEventListener(MouseEvent.CLICK, doBack);

btnRandom.addEventListener(MouseEvent.CLICK,
                             gotoRandomFrame);
```

The solution continues on the next page...

Solution – Using a timer (continued)

```
function doNext(event:Event):void
{
   // Reset the timer.
   timer.stop();
   timer.start();
   // Use an if statement to see if the...
   // ...current frame is the last frame.
   if (currentFrame == totalFrames)
   {
        // If on last frame go to frame 1.
        gotoAndStop( 1 );
   }
   else
   {
        // Go to the next frame.
        nextFrame();
   }
   // Update the user feedback.
   txtFeedback.text = String(currentFrame);
}
function doBack(event:Event):void
{
   // Reset the timer.
   timer.stop();
   timer.start();
   // If current frame is frame 1.
   if (currentFrame == 1)
   {
        // If on frame 1 go to last frame.
        gotoAndStop( totalFrames );
   }
   else
   {
        // Go to the previous frame.
        prevFrame();
   }
   // Update the user feedback.
   txtFeedback.text = String(currentFrame);
}
```

CHAPTER 5 – SIMPLER EVENT HANDLING

Overview

Understanding the ActionScript event model can save time and produce code that is simpler, easier to maintain and easier to read.

This chapter takes a deeper look at event handing. Properties of the event object will be used to simplify event handling.

Topics

- Event objects
- Event object properties
- Event flow
- The event's target
- The event's currentTarget
- Easier event handling

Event objects

Related file: The following file contains the examples for this discussion. [class files]/simplerEventHandlng/Example_eventObject.fla.

Objects generate events that are used to trigger functions called listeners or handlers. Objects pass their event handlers information about the event. The information is in the form of the properties of an event object.

The event object is much like any other object. It is a multivalued variable. It is a variable that contains other variables called properties. Some of its properties can be seen using a simple trace statement.

```
function eventHandler(event:Event):void
{
  trace(event);
}
```

The example above would produce a trace similar to the following sample.

```
[MouseEvent type="click" bubbles=true cancelable=false
eventPhase=2 localX=125 localY=17 stageX=125 stageY=17
relatedObject=null ctrlKey=false altKey=false
shiftKey=false delta=0]
```

The trace shows that the event object contains quite a bit of information. However some really useful properties of the event object do not show up in the trace. The useful properties are references to other objects. The information is there in the event object but simply does not show up in the trace.

Event object properties

Two important properties of the event object are target and currentTarget. The target is the object that generated the event. CurrentTarget is the name of the object the handler is assigned to.

In all of the examples so far the target and currentTarget have been the same. They do not need to be the same. This is the secret to simplifying event handling.

Since both the target and currentTarget properties are objects themselves tracing their value directly will return an object reference. Tracing event.target and event.currentTarget will produce results similar to those below.

- [object Stage]
- [object SimpleButton]
- [object someClip_8]

This object reference is all that is needed to refer back to the target object anonymously; without using the target's actual name. When needed, properties of target and currentTarget (such as name) can be explicitly traced out just like the properties of the event object.

Event flow

In the Flash player, some events move through the application. This allows event listeners to be set on objects other than the object that created the event. This creates a flexible event handling framework that allows simpler event handling.

The event flow starts at the root. Event objects start at the root of the movie and move through the application until they reach the object that generated the event. After reaching their target they move back through all the target's parents until they return to the root.

This creates three distinct phases to event propagation.

1. Capture phase
2. Target phase
3. Bubbling Phase

During the capture phase the event object moves from the root through all objects until it reaches the parent of the object that created the event.

This is why the object that generates the event is called the target. The target is the destination the event object is heading for as it moves through the application. By default, no listeners are called during the capture phase. Although the capture phase can be used to execute listeners this would be extremely unusual.

During the target phase any handlers assigned to the target execute.

During the bubbling phase the event object moves from the target back to the root of the application. This is when other listeners assigned to the event execute.

Simplifying event handling

Changing how handlers are assigned can simplify event handling. Instead of creating a handler for each button, buttons can be collected into a movieClip and one handler set on the movieClip holding the buttons.

Once a handler is set on the movieClip holding a group of buttons the handler needs to be able to respond differently to each button. The handler also needs to ignore unwanted events from the container. Unwanted events can come from mouse actions in the space between objects in the container clip or from interaction with background artwork in the container.

Responding to events

When one handler is used to handle events from multiple objects the handler usually needs to be able to produce different results for each object.

The key to accomplishing this is the event object's target property. The target property is always a reference to the object that created the event.

A unique response to an individual object can be created by using the object reference to the target, the target's name or extra information stored in the target.

Later in this chapter, buttons will be given the names of frame labels. The name of the selected button will be extracted from the event object and the playback head sent to that label.

Limiting event generation

When assigning a handler to a parent container it usually necessary to exclude the container itself from creating events. Clicking on an object in a container could generate two mouse events. One event because the child was clicked on and another event because the container the child is in was also clicked on. These would both trigger the handler assigned to the container causing it to execute twice.

The following expression will prevent the container from generating mouse events.

```
containerClip.mouseEnabled = false;
```

mouseEnabled affects the object it is applied to but not its children.

Another situation occurs when a sprite or movieClip has a text object inside. If the user clicks directly on the text object the text object blocks the mouse actions from the objects behind it. This prevents the handler from being triggered.

All of the children inside an object can be prevented from responding to the mouse. Events will only be generated by the parent of the children.

The following expression prevents all of the children of an object from generating mouse events.

```
mouseChildren = false;
```

This expression is not needed in this example. The mouseChildren property will be used later on in the chapter on movieClip buttons.

Simpler updates

Using one handler makes updates much simpler. To add more navigation new buttons having the correct names are simply added to the container clip.

Example – Event objects

File: [class files]/simplerEventHandlng/Example_eventObject.fla.

Overview

The example file demonstrates how events move through the application carrying information about the event with them. It demonstrates how event handling can be simplified using one handler for several buttons.

Suggestions

1. Open and examine the file. There are buttons and movieClips containing buttons on the stage. The movieClips are nested. ActionScript for event handling is in frame 1 of the main timeline. Some of the ActionScript is currently commented out. Only a handler that traces out the event object is active.
2. Run the file. Only a click on the red button causes a response. The click handler traces out some of the properties of the event object.
3. Examine the trace of the event object properties. Among a lot of other detailed information the type of the event is listed; a click. Some other key properties are not shown in this trace.
4. Comment out the trace of the event object.
5. Remove the comments from the next block of traces.
6. Run the file, click the red button and examine the trace. Because the handler is assigned to redButton and redButton is the object generating the event the properties event.target and event.currentTarget are the same.
7. Comment out the block of traces that just ran. Remove the comments from the next block of traces. The event object properties are concatenated with strings to make a more readable output.
8. Run the file to check the edits.
9. Comment out the listener for redButton and remove the comment from the line assigning stage as the listener.

10. Run the file and click on different places in the file. Observe the traces. (The output window can be cleared by right clicking and choosing Clear.) No matter where in the application the object being clicked on is, the stage hears and responds to all the clicks. The event target will change as different objects are clicked on. The current target, the object handling the event is always the stage. Notice that even when artwork is clicked on instead of a button an event is generated.

11. Comment out the listener assignment for the stage and remove the comment from the line assigning mcGreen as the listener.

12. Run the file again. Now clicks on the stage or mcBlue do nothing.

13. Remove the comments from the lines that set the mouseEnabled properties to false.

14. Run and test by clicking on objects. Now, only clicks on the buttons inside the movieClips generate events. Here the statements for setting mouseEnabled to false were issued in the main timeline. In other cases it might be more practical if each object carried those actions inside themselves.

Code – Event objects

```
// Add a listener to the redButton.
// redButton.addEventListener(MouseEvent.CLICK,
                                clickHandler);

// Add a listener to mcChild.
mcGreen.addEventListener(MouseEvent.CLICK,
                                clickHandler);

// Prevent stray clicks on artwork etc...
// ...from generating events.
mcGreen.mouseEnabled = false;

// One handler will respond to ALL of the events.
function clickHandler(event:Event):void
{

   trace(event);

   /*
   trace(event.type);
   trace(event.target);
   trace(event.target.name);
   trace(event.currentTarget);
   */

   trace("You did a " + event.type + " on: ")
   trace("An object - " + event.target + ".");
   trace("Named " + event.target.name + ".");
   trace("The object handling the event is: " +
         event.currentTarget + ".");
   trace(event.currentTarget + "'s name is " +
         event.currentTarget.name + ".");
   trace(".................");


}
```

Using Object Names in Handlers

Related file: No file. This short discussion leads right into an exercise.

Button names can be used to easily create frame based navigation. For navigation within a movieClip, buttons can simply be given the names of frame labels. Inside the handler the event target's name is used to provide the name of the frame to jump to.

```
gotoAndStop( event.target.name );
```

Using the name of the specific button provides a fast and simple method to create individual responses from different objects with one handler.

A more sophisticated technique does not rely on button names. It stores extra information in a special type of button. Later examples in this book will show how to create buttons that are based on movieClips. This will allow extra information to be stored in the movieClip buttons and remove dependence on using special button names.

MouseOver vs. RollOver

ActionScript has two events, MouseEvent.MOUSE_OVER and MouseEvent.ROLL_OVER, that are similar but have a key difference. MOUSE_OVER events bubble, they move through the application, ROLL_OVER events do not.

MOUSE_OVER events can be used to simplify event handling using a container clip. ROLL_OVER events must be written directly against the object creating the event.

Try it – Simpler handlers

Challenge

Use one listener assignment and one handler to respond to mouse over events from four different buttons. Have the movie jump to the keyframe that has the same frame label as the name of the button that the mouse is over. The solution to this challenge will be surprisingly simple, taking just a very few lines of code.

There is a suggestion for solving the challenge on this page. The following page offers a solution. A starter file has been provided.

Starter File

[class files]/simplerEventHandlng/Begin_simplerHandlers.fla.

The starter file is an ad banner. Close up views of cars appear at different frames along the timeline. Those frames have frames labels. The frame labels match the names of the four buttons on stage.

Suggestions

1. Open and examine the starter file.
2. Place the four buttons on the stage into one movieClip. The simplest way is to select all four buttons and use Convert to Symbol. The suggested instance name for this new movieClip is mcButtons.
   Note: The particular buttons used here may be hard to select. The buttons are outlines only. Clicking inside the button will not select it. The outline of the button must be clicked on.
3. Go to frame 1 of the actions layer and assign a mouse over handler to the newly created button container, mcButtons.
4. In the handler have the movie go to and stop on the frame that has the same label as the event target's name.
5. Test the movie. Notice that errors are being thrown when the mouse is moved over the button container and not the buttons.
6. Disable mouse events on the button holder so that only the buttons inside create mouse over events.
7. Test the movie again. The movie should now work without error.

Solution – Simpler handlers

Here is a solution without comments. It shows how little code is needed to control any number of buttons. Commented code is available in the bottom half of this page.

Frame 1 of the actions layer.

```
stop();

mcButtons.addEventListener(MouseEvent.MOUSE_OVER,
                           doMouseOver);

mcButtons.mouseEnabled = false;

function doMouseOver(event:Event):void
{
   gotoAndStop(event.target.name);
}
```

Commented code.

```
stop();

// Assign a listener to the button holder.
// Use the mouse over event.
mcButtons.addEventListener(MouseEvent.MOUSE_OVER,
                           doMouseOver);

// Stop the parent of the buttons...
// ...from generating mouse vents.
mcButtons.mouseEnabled = false;

// Write the handler.
function doMouseOver(event:Event):void
{
   // Go to the frame label that...
   // ...is the event target's name.
   gotoAndStop(event.target.name);
}
```

CHAPTER 6 – DRAGGING OBJECTS

Overview

The ability to drag objects is used in advanced interfaces and game development. ActionScript has a number of methods and properties that allow developers to manage the dragging of objects.

Topics

1. Dragging methods (startDrag(), stopDrag())
2. Creating custom cursors
3. Dragging properties (dropTarget)
4. The hitTestObject() method
5. Using movieClips as buttons
6. Creating a drag and match game

Dragging objects

ActionScript has methods and properties that easily allow users to drag objects. startDrag() begins the drag operation. stopDrag() releases, or drops, the object. The dropTarget property gives the name of the object the mouse was over when the dragged object was released.

The following example shows how to attach an object to the mouse.

```
someObject.startDrag();
```

If startDrag() is called without the mouse being over the object there will be an offset between the mouse and the dragged object. This offset can be removed by adding an argument to startDrag(). When the object is clicked on to start dragging it this argument is not needed. The mouse will already be on the object.

The next example aligns the objects registration point to the mouse. It sets the “’lockCenter” parameter to true, placing the object on the mouse.

```
someObject.startDrag(true);
```

Hiding the mouse cursor

Dragging an object provides a way to easily create custom cursors. In some cases the standard cursor is hidden when using a custom cursor.

The Mouse class has methods to show and hide the normal cursor. The Mouse class is a top level class like the Math class so these methods are called directly on the class. The methods are Mouse.show() and Mouse.hide(). These methods are intuitive and do to the normal cursor exactly what they sound like they do.

Example – Drag basics

File: [class files]/dragging/Example_dragBasics.fla

Overview

The example file demonstrates the basics of dragging objects. Dragging objects, attaching the dragged object to the mouse and hiding the system cursor are shown.

The example file has movieClip named mcCursor on the stage and actions in frame 1.

Suggestions

1. Open and run the file.
   - The custom cursor follows the mouse.
   - The cursor is offset from the mouse.
2. Examine the actions in frame 1 of the actions layer.
3. Change mcCursor.startDrag(); to mcCursor.startDrag(**true**);
4. Run the file again and notice that the custom cursor is aligned with the system cursor.
5. Remove the comments from the line Mouse.hide();
6. Run the file again and observe that system cursor is gone.

Code – Drag Basics

Frame 1 of the actions layer.

```
// Start dragging the cursor clip.
// Without arguments startDrag()...
// ...can produce an offset between...
// ...the mouse and the cursor.
// mcCursor.startDrag();
// Use the lock mouse to center argument...
// ... to center the clip's registration point...
// ...on the mouse position.
   mcCursor.startDrag(true);
// Hide the system cursor.
   Mouse.hide();
```

MovieClips as buttons

Most new Flash developers are familiar with simpleButtons. The SimpleButton class is exactly that; a class that allows users to very simply create interactive buttons. Buttons of the SimpleButton class have predefined frames that automatically activate in response to the mouse. All the buttons used in the examples and exercises so far have been of the SimpleButton class.

MovieClips can also be used as buttons. They can be used to create buttons that have more functionality than the SimpleButton class. They can also be used if only minimal functionality is needed.

One major limitation of the SimpleButton class is that there is no way to give simpleButton instances new properties. There is no way for a simpleButton to store extra data. Storing data in a button is a very powerful technique that will be used later in this chapter. An upcoming chapter will take a deeper look at using movieClips as buttons for advanced functionality.

buttonMode

By default, a movieClip being used as a button provides no feedback to the user that it is an interactive object. It does not automatically change state and the cursor does not automatically change to the hand icon as it does with a button.

Making the movieClip change states (up, over, down) when the mouse interacts with it is covered in detail in an upcoming chapter. It is easier than most people would think.

Showing the hand cursor when the mouse is over a movieClip is easy. This can be done by setting the movieClip's buttonMode property to true.

```
someMovieClip.buttonMode = true;
```

Disabling a movieClip button

It can be useful to disable a button at times. In the example of a drag game a developer may want to disable a button to indicate it is no longer used in game play.

A movieClip can be kept from interacting with the mouse by setting its mouseEnabled property to false.

```
someMovieClip.mouseEnabled = false;
```

dropTarget - (optional)

When an object is dropped a property called dropTarget is set in the dropped object. While this property can be very useful it is not as simple to use as it might sound. The value of dropTarget is not intuitive. It requires a bit of extra knowledge and work to be used effectively.

This example is provided as a reference to students because the effective use of dropTarget is not well documented. This discussion of the dropTarget property is provided in case the student needs help with this property at another time

The dropTarget property will not be used in the game that will be developed in this chapter. For many instructors and students it will be best to skip this example and move on to the discussion of hitTestbject.

DropTarget is useful when a developer needs to know what object an object was dropped on. If the developer already knows the object they want the user to drop an object on then hitTestObject() is a better choice. The hitTestObject() method is shown in the example after this.

One issue with dropTarget is that it only reports the object the mouse is over when the object is dropped. Even if it looks like the object being dropped is touching another object the dropTarget will be the object that the mouse was over.

Another issue with dropTarget is that its value will be that of a child in the container it was dropped on. Usually a developer wants to know the name of the container an object was dropped on.

A reference to the container an object was dropped on can be gotten by using dropTarget.parent. However dropTarget.parent has its own issues.

An attempt to use dropTarget or dropTarget.parent when the object is dropped on the empty stage will create errors. These are errors that come from trying to reference something that does not exist; a null object. The stage is the mother of all movieClips and has no parent.

If an object is dropped on the empty stage, that object's dropTarget will be null. This provides a simple way to avoid null object errors. An if statement can be used to be sure using dropTarget or dropTarget.parent will not produce errors.

```
// See if the dropped clip was actually over anything.
if (selectedObject.dropTarget)
{
   // Safe to use dropTarget.parent.
   var droppedOn:MovieClip =
         selectedObject.dropTarget.parent;
}
```

Example – dropTarget

File: [class files]/dragging/Example_dropTarget.fla

Overview

The example file demonstrates:

- Effectively using the dropTarget property.
- Using conditional logic to avoid throwing errors with dropTarget.

Three different mouseUp handlers are provided in this example. They will be assigned one after the other to the movieClip with the instance name redClip.

Finally, the movieClip will be set to show the hand cursor and then disabled from mouse interaction.

Suggestions

1. Open and run the file.
2. Drag and drop the red ball on an empty part of the movie.
3. Notice the output.
   dropTarget: null
   TypeError: Error #1009: Cannot access a property or method of a null object reference.
   at Example_dropTarget_fla::MainTimeline/showProblems()
4. Drop the red ball on a target (the blue circles).
5. Notice that:
   - If the tip of the system cursor is not over one of the targets the dropTarget is the stage.
   - When dropped on the stage the value of dropTarget is null.
   - It is the mouse position that sets dropTarget, not necessarily the object the ball is touching.
   - When the ball is dropped on the targets dropTarget does not return the instance name of the target. DropTarget returns the name of the objects inside the target. The target clip is the dropTarget's parent.

6. Examine the code in frame 1 of the actions layer.
   - The redClip's mouse up event is assigned to a listener named showProblems.
   - showProblems currently traces out the event object.
7. In showProblems, remove the comment from the lines:
   trace("dropTarget.name: " + event.target.dropTarget.name); and
   ```
   trace("dropTarget.parent.name: " +
           event.target.dropTarget.parent.name);
   ```
8. Run the file again, drag and drop the ball on the stage and the targets.
9. Observe the following:
   - If the ball is dropped on one of the targets dropTarget.parent.name returns the name of the target.
   - If the ball is dropped on stage dropTarget.parent.name produces errors. The stage does not have a parent or a name property.
10. Turn the current mouse up listener assignment into a comment.
    // redClip.addEventListener(MouseEvent.MOUSE_UP, showProblems);
11. Remove the comment from the next handler.
    redClip.addEventListener(MouseEvent.MOUSE_UP, useIfs);
12. Examine the useIfs handler.
13. Notice that an if statement is checking to see that if dropTarget exists. If the ball is dropped on the stage dropTarget will be null and the body of the if won't run. This prevents event.target.dropTarget.parent from throwing an error. If the ball is dropped on a target dropTarget is not null and the statements in the body of the if using event.target.dropTarget.parent run. The next example uses that if statement in a mouse up handler to center the ball on a target.
14. Turn the current mouse up listener assignment into a comment.
    // redClip.addEventListener(MouseEvent.MOUSE_UP, useIfs);

15. Remove the comment from the next mouse up listener assignment.
    redClip.addEventListener(MouseEvent.MOUSE_UP, ifInAction);

16. Run the file.
    - If the ball is dropped on the stage no errors are thrown.
    - If the ball is dropped on a target the expression event.target.dropTarget.parent works successfully to center the ball on any target.

17. To show the hand icon instead of the standard cursor when the mouse is over the ball remove the comment from this line near the top of the code:
    redClip.buttonMode = true;

18. To disable the ball from being dragged after it is dropped on a target remove the comment from this line in the ifInAction handler:
    event.target.mouseEnabled = false;

Code – dropTarget

```
// Show the hand cursor when over redClip;
// redClip.buttonMode = true;

// Assign handlers.
redClip.addEventListener(MouseEvent.MOUSE_DOWN,
doDrag);

redClip.addEventListener(MouseEvent.MOUSE_UP,
showProblems);
// redClip.addEventListener(MouseEvent.MOUSE_UP,
useIfs);
// redClip.addEventListener(MouseEvent.MOUSE_UP,
                                ifInAction);

// Handlers.
function doDrag(event:MouseEvent):void
{
   event.target.startDrag();
}

// This handler throws errors when the ball...
// ...is dropped on the empty stage.
function showProblems(event:Event):void
{
   event.target.stopDrag();
   trace("dropTarget: " + event.target.dropTarget);
   trace("dropTarget.name: " +
            event.target.dropTarget.name);
   trace("dropTarget.parent.name: " +
            event.target.dropTarget.parent.name);
}
```

Code continues on next page...

Code – dropTarget (continued)

```
// Conditional logic prevents errors.
function useIfs(event:Event):void
{
   event.target.stopDrag();
   // Only use drop target if it is not null.
   if (event.target.dropTarget)
   {
        trace("dropTarget: " +
event.target.dropTarget);
        trace("dropTarget name: " +
              event.target.dropTarget.name);
        trace("dropTarget.parent: " +
              event.target.dropTarget.parent);
        trace("dropTarget.parent.name: " +
              event.target.dropTarget.parent.name);
   }
   else
   {
        trace("The drop target is null")
   }
}

// Take action on the event target...
// ...only if there is a drop target.
function ifInAction (event:Event):void
{
   event.target.stopDrag();

   if (event.target.dropTarget)
   {
        // Stop redClip from responding to mouse.
        // event.target.mouseEnabled = false;
        // Center clip on its target.
        event.target.x = event.target.dropTarget.x;
        event.target.y = event.target.dropTarget.y;
   }
 }
```

Simplifying expressions

The following file contains the examples for this discussion.
Related file: [class files]/dragging/Example_betterDropping.fla

Sometimes event.target and other expressions are simplified to a single, simple variable. This can be done for several reasons.

Turning an expression into a simple variable with a descriptive name can provide clarity about what the expression represents.

```
var selectedClip:MovieClip = event.target as
MovieClip;
```

Notice that in this case the event.target must be cast to a movieClip to prevent errors. This is slightly different than the previous casting examples.

In the previous examples of casting one data type was turned into a new instance of another (i.e. a string to a number). In this example, the as operator is used to tell the compiler that the object can be successfully used in the expression. Even though the object appears to be of an incompatible data type to the complier.

The event target is, by default, a very generic data type; an Object. Using a generic data type for the event target makes it more versatile. It allows the target to be any one of a number of more specific data types. This is possible because those more specific data types (SimpleButton, MovieClip, Sprite, etc.) all descend from the basic class, Object.

Providing a meaningful name for an expression with a simple variable reduces typing. It also improves performance. It is faster to read a variable's value than to read the value of a property.

The trade off is that each extra variable takes up a little extra memory. If the variables are declared in a function they only exist while the function is running and then the memory they take up is reclaimed.

Typically, if an expression is only used once in a function, use it as an expression. If it will be used several times consider turning it into a variable.

Dropping off stage

If handlers are assigned to dragging objects the conventional way releasing the mouse when the dragged object is off stage causes problems. The object being dragged will not know that the mouse was released if the release happens while the object is off stage. This causes the object to get 'stuck' to the mouse. The dragged object will remain 'stuck' until the mouse is released while the object is on stage.

This problem can be demonstrated with the following file:
[class files]/dragging/Example_dropTarget.fla

If the objects in the example are dragged off stage and the mouse is released while off stage the drop handler is not called.

The solution to this problem is to use the stage as the listener for the drop handler. Even if the mouse appears off stage the stage object will 'hear' the event and trigger the handler.

Problems could occur if a user releases the mouse when they are not dragging something. In that case the drop handler would still be called, possibly producing errors.

The solution is to only assign the drop handler to the stage after dragging starts. The drop handler is assigned to the stage in the drag handler.

The drop handler is then removed using removeEventListener in the drop handler. This helps prevent possible errors.

Not applying the drop handler to the dragged object creates a problem. Event.target cannot be used in the drop handler. Event.target will be the stage if the mouse is released off stage during a drag. This could cause problems.

Instead a variable is used to keep track of the clip being dragged. The clip being dragged is assigned to that variable in the drag handler. The variable is then used in the drop handler.

Example – dropTarget

File: [class files]/dragging/Example_betterDropping.fla

Overview

The example file demonstrates handling the release of the mouse when a dragged object is off stage.

The drag and drop handlers have been rewritten to work even if the mouse is released off stage during a drag.

Suggestions

1. Open and run the file. Drag an object off stage and release the mouse. Notice that the object does not get 'stuck' to the mouse.
2. Examine the code in frame 1 of the actions layer.
3. Notice that the drag handler is assigned normally.
4. The drop handler is assigned to the stage in the drag handler.
5. The drop handler is removed in the drop handler.
6. A variable is used to keep track of the clip being dragged. The event target had to be cast to a MovieClip for the assignment to work.

Code – dropTarget

```
// Declare variables.
var selectedClip:MovieClip;
var startX:Number;
var startY:Number;

// Initialize the clips to show the hand cursor.
mcRectangle.buttonMode = true;
mcCircle.buttonMode = true;

// Assign handlers.
// Only handlers for drag are assigned here.
// Drop handler is assigned to stage after dragging
starts.
mcCircle.addEventListener(MouseEvent.MOUSE_DOWN,
doDrag);
mcRectangle.addEventListener(MouseEvent.MOUSE_DOWN,
doDrag);

// Handlers.
function doDrag(event:MouseEvent):void
{
   // Record which clip is being dragged.
   selectedClip = event.target as MovieClip;

   // Record starting position.
   startX = selectedClip.x;
   startY = selectedClip.y;

   // Start dragging.
   selectedClip.startDrag();

   // Add listener to stage for clip drop.
   stage.addEventListener(MouseEvent.MOUSE_UP,
doDrop);
}
```

Continued on next page...

Code – dropTarget (continued)

```
function doDrop(event:MouseEvent):void
{
   // Remove drop listener.
   stage.removeEventListener(MouseEvent.MOUSE_UP,
   doDrop);
   // Stop dragging.
   selectedClip.stopDrag();

   // Return to start position.
   selectedClip.x = startX;
   selectedClip.y = startY;
}
```

hitTestObject()

The hitTestObject method can be used to determine if two objects are touching. While the dropTarget property relies on the mouse position to determine the result, the hitTestObject method actually checks to see if two objects are touching on the screen.

Unlike dropTarget the hitTestObject method does not provide the names of the objects that are touching. The names must be provided to the hitTestObject method by the developer as literals or variables.

HitTestObject returns true if the two specified objects are touching and false if they are not. This makes hitTestObject() easy to use in an if statement.

```
if (thisObject.hitTestObject(thatObject))
{
    // Do something.
}
```

Example – hitTestObject()

File: [class files]/dragging/Example_hitTestObject.fla

Overview

This file shows how to match a dragged object to a specific target by using hitTestObject.

Suggestions

1. Open and run the file. The silver circle and the rectangle will only center on their corresponding target.
2. Examine the actions in frame 1 of the actions layer.
3. One handler is used to start dragging both objects.
4. Two separate handlers are used when dropping (stopping the dragging) of the objects. Each drop handler has a different hitTestObject expression. In these handlers the reference to the dropped clip is turned into a simple, easy to use variable.
5. Run the file again.
6. Drag an object until the mouse is off stage and release the mouse.
7. The dragged object becomes 'stuck' on the mouse. This happens because the mouse was not over the object being dragged. This will be fixed in the next example.

Code – hitTestObject()

```
// Initialize the clips to drag.
mcRectangle.buttonMode = true;
mcCircle.buttonMode = true;

// Assign handlers.
mcRectangle.addEventListener(MouseEvent.MOUSE_DOWN,
                             doDrag);
mcRectangle.addEventListener(MouseEvent.MOUSE_UP,
                              doDropRectangle);

mcCircle.addEventListener(MouseEvent.MOUSE_DOWN,
doDrag);
mcCircle.addEventListener(MouseEvent.MOUSE_UP,
                           doDropCircle);

// Handlers.
function doDrag(event:MouseEvent):void
{
   event.target.startDrag();
}

// Drop handler for mcRectangle.
function doDropRectangle(event:MouseEvent):void
{
var droppedClip:MovieClip = event.target as MovieClip;

   droppedClip.stopDrag();
   // If the dropped clip is touching...
   // ...the rectangle target.
   if (droppedClip.hitTestObject(rectangleTarget))
   {
        // Disable the dropped clip.
        droppedClip.mouseEnabled = false;
        // Center the dropped clip on target.
        droppedClip.x = rectangleTarget.x;
        droppedClip.y = rectangleTarget.y;
   }
}
```

Code continues on next page...

Code – hitTestObject() (continued)

```
// Drop handler for mcCircle.
function doDropCircle(event:MouseEvent):void
{
   var droppedClip:MovieClip = event.target as
MovieClip;

   droppedClip.stopDrag();
   // If the dropped clip is touching...
   // ...the circle target.
   if (droppedClip.hitTestObject(circleTarget))
   {
          // Disable the dropped clip.
         droppedClip.mouseEnabled = false;
         // Center the dropped clip on target.
         droppedClip.x = circleTarget.x;
         droppedClip.y = circleTarget.y;
   }
}
```

Adding properties to objects

Related file: The following file contains the examples for this discussion. [class files]/dragging/Example_propertiesFrontEvents.fla.

Properties are simply variables in an object. Adding new properties to objects allows the objects to carry important information with them.

The class often used for buttons is the simpleButton class. New properties cannot be added to simpleButtons. A class that cannot have new properties added to its instances is referred to as a sealed class.

Dynamic classes are classes that can have new properties arbitrarily added to them. The MovieClip class is a dynamic class. This is one of several reasons using movieClips as buttons can be better than using buttons built from the SimpleButton class.

Properties can be added to a movieClip to hold useful information such as the name of a file to load, a frame label to go to, or a target for the clip to hit.

```
someObject.someNewProperty = someValue;
```

Properties that are added dynamically do not use the var keyword. There is no simple, direct way to impose data typing on dynamically added properties.

Simplifying event handling

In a drag game each game piece that will be dragged can be given a property representing the target it should be dropped on.

```
someClip.clipToHit = mcSomeTarget;
```

This simplifies event handling. It also frees the developer from depending on special instance names as was done in the previous chapter.

Instead of having to write a separate handler for each object with that object's target hard coded into the handler, one handler can be written to handle all the game pieces. The name of the object the game piece should be dropped on can be extracted from the event target in the handler.

The following example assumes a movieClip has been given a new property: clipToHit.

```
var droppedClip:MovieClip = event.target as MovieClip;
var targetClip:MovieClip = droppedClip.clipToHit;
```

Bringing an object to the font

It is a common practice to bring the object being dragged to the front of other objects during dragging. In most cases, users will not want to see the object they are dragging pass behind other objects.

Bringing the object being dragged to the front will also prevent a problem that can occur when handlers are being shared by multiple objects. If the object being dragged is behind another interactive object when the mouse is released the dragged object's handler may not be called. The mouse event will be blocked by the object in front.

The display list

The Flash player keeps track of objects being drawn on the screen in special lists called display lists. Each visible object has its own display list. All visual objects are a child of their parent's display list. An object's position in a display list can be changed to bring it to the front. An object can even be moved from one display list to another.

To bring an object to the front simply add it back into the display with the addChild method.

```
addChild( objectToBringTofront );
```

It is possible to move an object from inside of one object to another by adding the object to another object's display list. This can have unexpected results. If the two objects' coordinate systems (registration points) are not aligned the object may appear to jump on screen when moved to a different display list.

When using the event target with addChild and the event target is a movieClip the event target will need to be cast to a MovieClip for addChild() to work without error.

Simplifying event handling

Event handling can be simplified using the technique learned in the last chapter. All of the game pieces to be dragged can be placed inside a movieClip. The handler can be assigned to the container holding the game pieces instead of being assigned to each individual game piece.

If addChild() is used to bring the game piece to the front during dragging the game piece should usually kept in the container it is in.

Assuming this code is in the main timeline, it brings an object to the front of other objects in the clip holder.

```
clipHolder.addChild(event.target as MovieClip);
```

Instead of moving it to the main timeline.

```
addChild(event.target as MovieClip);
```

Moving an object from the display list of the object it is in to another object may cause two things to happen. The object's position may jump and any handlers assigned to that object may quit working.

The object may jump because it will be moved to a different coordinate system. The handler may stop working because the object is outside of the container that had a listener assigned to it. This can actually be handy when the dragged object is dropped on its target in a matching game.

If a game piece is removed from its container and added as a child of the main timeline it is in the right coordinate system to be easily centered on a target in the main timeline. Just match the x and y of the game piece to the target's. The fact that the game piece's handler has stopped working is a good thing. If the game piece is on target there is no need for the handler to keep working.

Example – Properties, bring to front and simpler events

File: [class files]/dragging/Example_propertiesFrontEvents.fla.

Overview

This example file demonstrates:

- Creating and using new properties in movieClips
- Bringing objects to the front
- Simplifying event handling

Suggestions

1. Open and examine the file. Examine the clipHolder movieClip on the stage. It holds three movieClips; clip1, clip2 and clip3.
2. Run the file. Click on the clips.

   A trace action prints information to the screen. The selected clip comes to the front when clicked on. The selected clip jumps out of position. Further clicks on that object produce no new traces.
3. Examine the actions in frame 1 of the actions layer.

   Each movieClip in clipHolder is given a new property: extraData. The extraData property is traced from the event target in the handler. In the handler the addChild method is adding the selected object to the main timeline's display list instead of the clipHolder's display list. This is causing the clip to jump and to stop calling responding to handlers set on clipHolder.
4. Change the addChild method so that the event target is added back into clipHolder. This can be done by editing the line with addChild or commenting that line out and removing the comment for the statement a few lines further down the code.

```
addChild(event.target as MovieClip);
```

6. Now when an object is clicked on it stays in place and the handlers continue to be called.

Code – hitTestObject()

```
// Add some properties to the clips...
// ...inside the clip holder.
clipHolder.clip1.extraData = "plaid";
clipHolder.clip2.extraData = "checkered";
clipHolder.clip3.extraData = "paisley";

// Assign handler.
clipHolder.addEventListener(MouseEvent.CLICK,
                            clickHandler);

// Handler.
function clickHandler(event:MouseEvent):void
{
   // Move the target from the...
   // ...clipHolder's display list to the...
   // ...front of the main timeline's display list.
   // addChild(event.target as MovieClip);
   // Bring the target to the front of...
   // ... the clipHolder's display list.
   clipHolder.addChild(event.target as MovieClip);
   // Retrieve the information in the dynamic
property.
   trace(event.target.extraData);
}
```

Issues with using a container for movieClips

Related file: This discussion leads right into an exercise.

Issues arise with game pieces in a container clip when the developer tries to put the game piece on the center of a target in the main timeline. If the x and y position of the target in the main time line are read and applied to the dropped clip inside the container clip it will probably not align with the target. This is because the dropped clip is in a different coordinate system from the target clip. The two coordinate systems are probably not aligned. The coordinates from one system cannot be used directly in the other.

There are several possible ways to address this issue.

One simple, direct way would be to align the coordinate systems of the container clip and the main timeline. The origin (center) of the main timeline's coordinate system is the upper left hand corner of the stage. If the container clip's registration point is placed in the upper left corner of the stage the dropped clip can be simply aligned with its target.

```
droppedClip.x = targetClip.x;
droppedClip.y = targetClip.y;
```

A similar, but more elegant approach that does not require moving the container clip's position is to move the dropped clip to the main timeline after it has hit its target. Once the dropped clip is in the same object as its target it can simply and directly be aligned with its target. Moving the dropped object from its container has the added benefit of disabling the handler on the game piece. It will be outside of the container that is responding to the mouse actions.

However, moving the dropped clip to the main timeline will cause the remaining game pieces to pass behind the clip in the main timeline. This can be corrected by bringing the container clip to the front of the main timeline. This is accomplished by adding the container clip back to the main timeline, placing it in front of everything.

This sample would be in the main timeline.

```
// Move the dropped clip from…
// …any container it is in…
// …and place it in main timeline.
// Bring dropped clip to front.
addChild(droppedClip);
// Bring container clip to front.
addChild(containerClip);
// Align clip with target.
droppedClip.x = targetClip.x;
droppedClip.y = targetClip.y;
```

The example above will generally be the best choice.

Another less elegant, but simple approach would be to leave the dropped clip in the container and compensate mathematically for the offset in registration points. This can be done by subtracting the container clip's position from the target's position.

```
droppedClip.x = targetClip.x - mcContainer.x;
droppedClip.y = targetClip.y - mcContainer.y;
```

Dropping outside the stage

As seen in a previous example, there is a problem when the mouse is released outside of the stage while dragging an object. The mouse up handler is not triggered if the mouse is off stage. The stopDrag() method is not executed. This causes the object being dragged to get 'stuck' to the mouse until the mouse is pressed and released again.

This problem can be fixed by using the stage as the object listening for the mouse up event. A listener assigned to the stage will 'hear' the mouse go up even if it is off stage.

The listener for the mouse up can be assigned to the stage in the same way a listener is assigned to any other object. However, assigning a listener to the stage and managing it the usual way can create problems.

When a listener for the mouse up event is assigned to the stage it will trigger its handler anytime the mouse goes up anywhere. It will not matter if an object is being dragged or not, the mouse up handler will be triggered. This unnecessary calling of the mouse up handler could cause problems. There would definitely be problems if certain properties from the event object are used in the handler. Extra variables that have been added to the clips being dragged would not be available in the handler when the target of the event is the stage. This would cause Flash to throw errors.

The solution is to use the mouse down handler to assign the mouse up listener to the stage. Then when mouse up is called the listener for the stage is removed. This way the mouse up handler for the stage is only active during the dragging process.

Assigning a listener to the stage

The following sample shows the correct assignment of listeners for robust dragging. The function listening for the event to start dragging is unconditionally assigned. The function listening for the release is assigned to the stage after the dragging starts. It is removed after the object is released and it is no longer needed.

Since the listener for the release is assigned to the stage the event object cannot be used to reference the clip being dragged. Instead a variable is created outside of the handlers. The drag handler sets the variable to the clip being dragged. The drop handler then uses that variable to know which clip to act on.

```
// A variable to hold the clip being used.
var selectedClip:MovieClip;

// Mouse down calls doDrag.
someClip.addEventListener(MouseEvent.MOUSE_DOWN,
doDrag);

// Handlers

function doDrag(event:MouseEvent):void
{
   stage.addEventListener(MouseEvent.MOUSE_UP,
   doDrop);
   selectedClip = event.target as MovieClip;
   selectedClip.startDrag();
   // Do other stuff
}

// When the selected clip is dropped.
function doDrop(event:MouseEvent):void
{
   selectedClip.stopDrag();
   // Remove the listener from the stage.
   stage.removeEventListener(MouseEvent.MOUSE_UP,
   doDrop);
   // Do other stuff
}
```

Try it – A drag and match game

Challenge

Create a game where users must drag game pieces onto a corresponding target. If the user misses the target have the target jump back to where it came from. Display some feedback after the user has matched all the game pieces to their target.

There is a suggestion for solving the challenge on this page. A solution is offered following the challenge. Two types of starter files have been provided.

Starter Files

Two different starting files are provided. Each file offers a different level of challenge. Choose the level that is the most comfortable for you

> **Challenging** - This file has a few comments to help.
> [class files]/dragging/Begin_dragGame.fla.
>
> **Fill in the blanks** - The skeleton of the code is provided. Three question marks (???) have been placed everywhere more information is needed. The missing information can be found in the examples in this chapter.
> [class files]/dragging/Begin_dragGame_FillInTheBlanks.fla.

All the starter files contain all the needed movieClips for the game. They already have instance names and are placed on stage.

Suggestions

1. Declare two variables to hold the starting position of clip being dragged.
2. Declare a variable to store the name of the clip being dragged and dropped.
3. Set mcIcons buttonMode to true.
4. In frame 1 of the main timeline add properties to the game pieces inside mcIcons. The properties will hold the names of the clips they should hit. The three game pieces are: mcChicago, mcNyc & mcWdc. The three targets are: mcChicagoTarget, mcNycTarget, mcWdcTarget.

5. Assign a listener to mcIcons to start dragging a game piece when it is clicked on.
6. Write a function to handle dragging.
7. Inside the function for dragging:
    a. Assign the listener that will stop dragging the game piece when the mouse goes up. Assign this mouseUp listener to the stage.
    b. Use the event target to create a variable that holds a reference to the selected clip. Remember to cast it to a MovieClip.
    c. Record the selected clip's original starting position using the variable created in step 1.
    d. Bring the selected clip to the front of its container.
    e. Start dragging the selected clip.
8. Write the function to handle the release (or drop) of the game piece.
9. Inside the function for dropping:
    a. Stop dragging the selected clip.
    b. Remove the listener from the stage.
    c. Create a variable to hold the reference to the selected clip's target. Get the reference from the extra data that was added to the game piece.
    d. Use hitTestObject and an if statement to see if the selected clip hit the correct target.
    e. If the selected clip hit the target; move the selected clip to the main timeline, put the selected clip on its target and bring the clip with the game pieces in front of everything.
    f. If the selected clip missed the target put the selected clip back where it started.

SOLUTION – A drag and match game

File: [class files]/draggingObjects/Solution_dragGame.fla

The code for the solution is presented on the next few pages with and without comments.

```
var originalX:Number;
var originalY:Number;
var selectedClip:MovieClip;
mcIcons.mcChicago.clipToHit = mcChicagoTarget;
mcIcons.mcNyc.clipToHit = mcNycTarget;
mcIcons.mcWdc.clipToHit = mcWdcTarget;
mcIcons.addEventListener(MouseEvent.MOUSE_DOWN,
doDrag);
stage.addEventListener(MouseEvent.MOUSE_UP, doDrop);

function doDrag(event:MouseEvent):void
{
   selectedClip = event.target as MovieClip;
   originalX = selectedClip.x;
   originalY = selectedClip.y;
   mcIcons.addChild(selectedClip);
   selectedClip.startDrag();
}
function doDrop(event:MouseEvent):void
{
   selectedClip.stopDrag();
   var targetClip:MovieClip = selectedClip.clipToHit;
   if ( selectedClip.hitTestObject( targetClip ) )
   {
        addChild(selectedClip);
        addChild(mcIcons);
        selectedClip.x = targetClip.x;
        selectedClip.y = targetClip.y;
   }
   else
   {
        selectedClip.x = originalX ;
        selectedClip.y = originalY;
   }
}
```

SOLUTION – A drag and match game (continued)

```
// Declare two variables to hold...
// ...the game piece starting position.
var originalX:Number;
var originalY:Number;

// Variable to hold clip being dragged and dropped.
var selectedClip:MovieClip;

// Add properties to the game pieces.
// The properties will contain a reference...
// ...to the clips they should hit.
mcIcons.mcChicago.clipToHit = mcChicagoTarget;
mcIcons.mcNyc.clipToHit = mcNycTarget;
mcIcons.mcWdc.clipToHit = mcWdcTarget;

// Assign listener to clip holding game pieces.
// Mouse down calls doDrag.
mcIcons.addEventListener(MouseEvent.MOUSE_DOWN,
doDrag);

function doDrag(event:MouseEvent):void
{
   // Assign listener to mouse up for doDrop.
   // Adding listener to the stage allows drops...
   // ...when mouse is off stage to work properly.
   stage.addEventListener(MouseEvent.MOUSE_UP,
   doDrop);
   // Use the event target to create a variable...
   // ...that holds a reference to the selected clip.
   // Cast it to a MovieClip.
   selectedClip = event.target as MovieClip;
   // Record the clip's original starting position.
   originalX = selectedClip.x;
   originalY = selectedClip.y;
   // Bring the clip to the front of its container.
   mcIcons.addChild(selectedClip);
   // Start dragging.
   selectedClip.startDrag();
}
```

SOLUTION – A drag and match game (continued)

```
// When the selected clip is dropped.
function doDrop(event:MouseEvent):void
{
   // Stop dragging the selected clip.
        selectedClip.stopDrag();

   // Remove the listener from the stage.
   stage.removeEventListener(MouseEvent.MOUSE_UP,
doDrop);

   // Create a variable to reference...
   // ...the selected clip's clip to hit.
   var targetClip:MovieClip = selectedClip.clipToHit;

   // See if the selected clip hit the correct target.
   if ( selectedClip.hitTestObject( targetClip ) )
   {
        // Move selected clip to the main timeline.
        addChild(selectedClip);
        // Put the selected clip on its target.
        selectedClip.x = targetClip.x;
        selectedClip.y = targetClip.y;
        // Bring game pieces in front
        // of dropped piece.
        addChild(mcIcons);
   }
   else
   {
        // Put the selected clip back
        // where it started.
        selectedClip.x = originalX ;
        selectedClip.y = originalY;
   }
}
```

CHAPTER 7 – TWEENING AND EASING

Overview

The Tween class provides programmers with a way to change an object's properties over time. This can be used to create animation. The easing classes provide a way to modify the rate at which properties change. This creates acceleration, deceleration and other effects.

The width and heights of animated objects often need to be taken into consideration when using the Tween class.

Tweening and easing will be examined and then applied to the drag and match game.

Topics

- Importing classes
- Tween classes
- Easing functions
- Tween properties
- Tween methods
- Tween events

Importing Tween and Easing classes

Related file: The following file contains the examples for this discussion. [class files]/tweening/Example_tweeningBasics.fla.

The Tween and Easing classes are not a standard part of the Flash player. There are part of a large number of ActionScript classes that are not built into the player. These classes are kept external to keep the download size of the player small.

When these extra classes are needed they are added to the SWF. They are made available by using import statements. . They are then automatically compiled into the SWF when they are used. Imports should be the first thing in the code. This makes sure the imported classes are available to the rest of the code.

Unlike the optional imports for many event classes the Tweening and Easing classes must be imported.

The following two imports make the Tween class and all of the easing classes available.

```
import fl.transitions.Tween;
import fl.transitions.easing.*
```

Classes are stored in directories referred to as packages. The Tween class is kept inside a directory called transitions inside a directory called fl. Only the Tween class is being imported from fl.transitions. It is the only class needed from that package.

All of the classes from the fl.transitions.easing package are being imported. There are several Easing classes that can be used. Using the wildcard operator (*) at the end of the path makes all of the classes in that package available.

Only classes actually used in the code will end up being compiled into the SWF.

Tween parameters

The Tween class needs a number of parameters to operate. Only the last parameter is optional.

Here are the parameter names that ActionScript uses.

```
Tween(obj,prop,func,begin,finish,duration,useSeconds)
```

The following list explains each of the parameters.

- **obj**:Object
  Object that the Tween targets.
- **prop**:String
  Name of the property that will be affected.
- **func**:Function
  Name of the easing function to use.
- **begin**:Number
  The starting value for the property being tweened.
- **finish**:Number
  The ending value of the property being tweened.

- **duration**:Number
  Length of time of the for tween; set to infinity if negative or omitted.
- **useSeconds**:Boolean (Optional: default = false, use frames for duration.)
  A flag specifying whether to use seconds to calculate duration instead of frames. The function uses seconds to calculate duration if true or frames if false.

The parameter names are fairly straight forward but there are quite a few parameters. When the parameters are supplied with simple values can they are reasonably readable. When the values are the results of calculations, doing the calculations straight in the arguments can create code that is hard to read.

Consider the following example.

```
new Tween(event.target, "y", Regular.easeIn,
          event.target.y, stage.stageHeight -
          event.target.height;, 30);
```

Turning some of the parameter values in the previous example into variables can produce clearer code.

Working with many parameters

When using a new class with many parameters there is a trick that can make learning the new parameters easier. The parameters are broken out into clearly named variables and the variables are applied as arguments.

The variables create a little extra overhead in memory. If they are declared in a function like an event handler they are automatically removed from memory after the function is finished running.

```
var objectToTween:Object = mcBall;
var propertyToTween:String = "y";
var easingFunction:Function = None.easeNone;
var startValue:Number = objectToTween.y;
var endValue:Number = stage.stageHeight;
var duration:Number = 24;
var useSeconds:Boolean = false;

var tween:Tween = new Tween(objectToTween,
                            propertyToTween,
                            easingFunction,
                            startValue,
                            endValue,
                            duration,
                            useSeconds);
```

The original names for the parameters were fairly clear. The new names are very clear.

A good balance of techniques is to assign simple values to parameters directly in the arguments. Then create variables for the values that have to be calculated. That technique will be used in later examples.

While arguments are usually written one after the other, they can be written on separate lines as shown above. This is done to improve readability or to assist printing readable documentation.

Example – Tweening basics

File: [class files]/tweening/Example_tweeningBasics.fla

Overview

Tween parameters have been turned into variables. A tween is created using those variables. The values of some of the parameters/variables will be changed to produce different animations.

Suggestions

1. Open and examine the file.
    - A movieClip named mcBall is on the stage.
    - There are actions in frame 1 of the actions layer.
2. Run the file. The ball moves from its position near the top of the stage and travels down the stage and out of sight at the bottom.
3. Examine the actions in frame 1 of the actions layer.
4. The parameters change the value of mcBall's y property from where it currently is on the stage to the bottom edge of the screen. The ball's registration point is at the top of the ball. This causes the ball to move past the bottom of the screen before it stops.
5. To stop the ball at the bottom edge of the screen change the value of endValue. Subtract the ball's height from the stage height.
6. Modify the code and test. The ball stops on stage at the bottom of the stage instead of going past.
7. Change the easing by commenting out the current easingFunction and removing the comment from the next line. Run and observe the results. Strong.easeIn causes the ball to accelerate and then stop suddenly. Try Strong.easeOut and Strong.easeInOut.
8. Modify the code to make the ball fade out.
    - Change propertyToTween to alpha.
    - Change startValue to 1.
    - Change endValue to 0.

- Change the duration.
- Try using seconds instead of frames.

9. Run the file. The ball fades out.

Code – Tweening basics

```
import fl.transitions.Tween;
import fl.transitions.easing.*;

var objectToTween:Object = mcBall;
var propertyToTween:String = "y";
//  var propertyToTween:String = "alpha";
var easingFunction:Function = None.easeNone;
// var easingFunction:Function = Strong.easeInOut;
var startValue:Number = objectToTween.y;
// var startValue:Number = 1;
var endValue:Number = stage.stageHeight;
// var endValue:Number = stage.stageHeight -
   objectToTween.height;
// var endValue:Number = 0;
var duration:Number = 24;
// Default: useSeconds = false...
// ...counts duration in frames.
var useSeconds:Boolean = false;

var tween:Tween = new Tween(objectToTween,
                            propertyToTween,
                            easingFunction,
                            startValue,
                            endValue,
                            duration,
                            useSeconds);
```

Easing

Related file: The following file contains the examples for this discussion. [class files]/tweening/Example_easing.fla.

Easing describes a change in a property's value that is not constant. The change can speed up, slow down or appear to bounce. Easing is generally more apparent when used with motion.

An easing class and function must be provided to a tween. The parameter name for the easing class is func, but the argument expects both an easing class and an easing method from that class

The following example shows the general form of an easing expression. An expression of this form must be passed to the func parameter.

```
SomeEaseClass.someEaseFunction
```

The class sets the type of easing and the function determines when it is applied to the easing; at the beginning, at the end, at the beginning and end or not at all.

Not all combinations of tweens and easings will produce attractive motion.

The following are some specific examples of easing expressions.

```
Regular.easeInOut
Bounce.easeOut
Back.easeIn
None.easeNone
```

The following is a list of the easing classes and what they are used for.

Back
Object appears to initially move backwards at the beginning, end or both.

Bounce
Appears similar to a ball falling and bouncing on a floor with several decaying rebounds. Usually applied at the end of motion using easeOut

Elastic
The motion is defined by an exponentially decaying sine wave. The

appearance is similar to back but the object oscillates, moves both back and forth, at either or both ends of the animation.

None
The None class defines liner, un-accelerated motion.

The None class is used when no easing is needed. Its primary purpose is to provide a starting point and a shell for developers to use when they want to write their own easing functions. The None Tween class has a special easing function called easeNone that is used to clearly indicate that no easing is being applied.

Regular
The Regular class defines three easing functions to implement accelerated or decelerated motion. It accelerates using easeIn. It decelerates using easeOut. It does both with easeInOut.

Strong
Similar to Regular but more pronounced.

Each easing class has three or more functions that determine when the easing occurs.

The following is a list of the easing functions that all easing classes support.

easeIn
Applied at the beginning of the tween.

easeOut
Applied at the end of the tween.

easeInOut
Applied at the beginning and the end of the tween.

Looping

A tween can be played repeatedly by setting its looping property to true.

```
tween.looping = true;
```

Example – Easing

File: [class files]/tweening/Example_easing.fla.

Overview

This example file demonstrates the easing classes and functions.

It provides a handy visual reference to the different eases.

A variety of tweens have been created to demonstrate different tween and easing types.

Balls are used to provide demonstrations of motion. Squares have been provided to provide demonstrations of rotation and transparency.

The easing types are grouped together; easeIn, easeOut, and easeInOut.

Suggestions

1. Open and run the file. Click on the balls and squares.
2. Observe and compare the different motion that the different easing classes produce.
3. Examine the actions in frame 1 of the actions layer.
4. See what types of motion the different Tween classes and easing classes produce. Change the commented tweens in the ball handlers. Simply turn the current tween into a comment and uncomment the next tween in the list.
5. The commented out tweens in the square handlers will need easing classes added to them before they will run.

Code – Easing

```
import fl.transitions.easing.*;
import fl.transitions.*;

ball1.addEventListener(MouseEvent.CLICK, doBall1);
ball2.addEventListener(MouseEvent.CLICK, doBall2);
ball3.addEventListener(MouseEvent.CLICK, doBall3);

square1.addEventListener(MouseEvent.CLICK, doSquare1);
square2.addEventListener(MouseEvent.CLICK, doSquare2);

var topOfStage:Number = 20;
var bottomOfStage:Number =
        stage.stageHeight - ball1.height - 20;
// The duration can be overwritten in any handler.
// Just declare a new var duration inside habdler.
var duration:Number = 30;
```

Code continues on the next page...

Code continues on the next page...

Code – Easing (continued)

```
function doBall1(event:Event):void {
   var startValue:Number
   var finishValue:Number

   if (event.target.y == topOfStage)  {
         startValue = topOfStage;
         finishValue = bottomOfStage;
   }else{
         startValue = bottomOfStage;
         finishValue = topOfStage;
   }
   var tween:Tween = new Tween(event.target, "y",
    Regular.easeIn, startValue, finishValue,
    duration);
   // var tween:Tween = new Tween(event.target, "y",
        Strong.easeIn, startValue, finishValue,
        duration);

// var tween:Tween = new Tween(event.target, "y",
        Back.easeIn, startValue, finishValue,
    duration);
   // var tween:Tween = new Tween(event.target, "y",
        Bounce.easeIn, startValue, finishValue,
        duration);
   // var tween:Tween = new Tween(event.target, "y",
        Elastic.easeIn, startValue, finishValue,
         duration);
   // var tween:Tween = new Tween(event.target, "y",
        None.easeIn, startValue, finishValue,
        duration);
   // tween.looping = true;
}
```

Code continues on the next page…

Code – Easing (continued)

```
function doBall2(event:Event):void
{
   var startValue:Number
   var finishValue:Number

   if (event.target.y == topOfStage)
   {
         startValue = topOfStage;
         finishValue = bottomOfStage;
   }
   else
   {
         startValue = bottomOfStage;
         finishValue = topOfStage;
   }

var tween:Tween = new Tween(event.target, "y",
       Regular.easeOut, startValue, finishValue,
duration);
   // var tween:Tween = new Tween(event.target, "y",
      Strong.easeOut, startValue, finishValue,
duration);
   // var tween:Tween = new Tween(event.target, "y",
      Back.easeOut, startValue, finishValue,
duration);
   // var tween:Tween = new Tween(event.target, "y",
      Bounce.easeOut, startValue, finishValue,
duration);
   // var tween:Tween = new Tween(event.target, "y",
      Elastic.easeOut, startValue, finishValue,
duration);
   // var tween:Tween = new Tween(event.target, "y",
      None.easeOut, startValue, finishValue,
duration);
   // tween.looping = true;
}
```

Code continues on the next page…

Code – Easing (continued)

```
function doBall3(event:Event):void
{
   var startValue:Number
   var finishValue:Number

   if (event.target.y == topOfStage)
   {
         startValue = topOfStage;
         finishValue = bottomOfStage;
   }
   else
   {
         startValue = bottomOfStage;
         finishValue = topOfStage;
   }
   var tween:Tween = new Tween(event.target, "y",
   Regular.easeInOut, startValue, finishValue,
duration);
   // var tween:Tween = new Tween(event.target, "y",
      Strong.easeInOut, startValue, finishValue,
duration);
   // var tween:Tween = new Tween(event.target, "y",
      Back.easeInOut, startValue, finishValue,
duration);
   // var tween:Tween = new Tween(event.target, "y",
      Bounce.easeInOut, startValue, finishValue,
duration);
   // var tween:Tween = new Tween(event.target, "y",
      Elastic.easeInOut, startValue,
finishValue,duration);
   // var tween:Tween = new Tween(event.target, "y",
      None.easeInOut, startValue, finishValue,
duration);
   // tween.looping = true;
}
```

Code continues on the next page...

Code – Easing (continued)

```
function doSquare1(event:Event):void
{
   // Override duration with a local var.
   var duration:Number = 100;
   var startValue:Number = 0;
   var finishValue:Number = 360;
   // !!! Supply an easing type if you use any of the
      commented examples below.
   // easeIn, easeOut or easeInOut.
   // var tween:Tween = new Tween(event.target,
"rotation",
      Regular.???, startValue, finishValue, duration);
   // var tween:Tween = new Tween(event.target,
"rotation",
      Strong.???, startValue, finishValue, duration);
   // var tween:Tween = new Tween(event.target,
"rotation",
      Back.???, startValue, finishValue, duration);
   // var tween:Tween = new Tween(event.target,
"rotation",
      Bounce.???, startValue, finishValue, duration);
   // var tween:Tween = new Tween(event.target,
"rotation",
      Elastic.???, startValue, finishValue, duration);
   var tween:Tween = new Tween(event.target,
"rotation",
   None.easeNone, startValue, finishValue, duration);
   // tween.looping = true;
}
```

Code continues on the next page...

Code – Easing

```
function doSquare2(event:Event):void
{
   // Override duration with a local var.
   var duration:Number = 50;
   var startValue:Number = event.target.alpha;
   var finishValue:Number = 0;
   // !!! Supply an easing type if you use any of the
      commented examples below.
   // var tween:Tween = new Tween(event.target,
"alpha",
      Regular.???, startValue, finishValue, duration);
   // var tween:Tween = new Tween(event.target,
"alpha",
      Strong.???, startValue, finishValue, duration);
   // var tween:Tween = new Tween(event.target,
"alpha",
      Back.???, startValue, finishValue, duration);
   // var tween:Tween = new Tween(event.target,
"alpha",
      Bounce.???, startValue, finishValue, duration);
   // var tween:Tween = new Tween(event.target,
"alpha",
      Elastic.???, startValue, finishValue, duration);
   var tween:Tween = new Tween(event.target, "alpha",
   None.easeNone, startValue, finishValue, duration);
}
```

Tween methods

Related file: The following file contains the examples for this discussion. [class files]/tweening/Example_tweenEvents.fla.

The tween methods provide a full set of tools for controlling tweens.

The following is a list of tween methods and what they do.

continueTo(finish:Number,duration:Number)
Instructs the tweened animation to continue tweening from its current animation point to a new finish and duration point.

fforward()
Forwards the tweened animation directly to the final value of the tweened animation.

nextFrame()
Forwards the tweened animation to the next frame of an animation that was stopped.

prevFrame()
Plays the previous frame of the tweened animation from the current stopping point of an animation that was stopped.

resume()
Resumes the play of a tweened animation that has been stopped.

rewind(t:Number=0)
Moves the play of a tweened animation back to its starting value.

start()
Starts the play of a tweened animation from its starting point.

stop()
Stops the play of a tweened animation at its current value.

yoyo()
Instructs the tweened animation to play in reverse from its last direction. The tween should be finished before calling yoyo().

Tween events

Tweens generate events. Complex animations can be created using these events to trigger new tweens. The following is a list of tween events.

motionChange
Indicates the tween has changed and screen has been updated.

motionFinish
Indicates that the tween has reached the end and finished.

motionLoop
Indicates that the tween restarted playing from the beginning in looping mode.

motionResume
Indicates that the tween has resumed playing after being paused.

motionStart
Indicates that the tween motion has started playing.

motionStop
Indicates that the tween has been stopped with an explicit call to Tween.stop().

The motionFinish event is very useful for triggering a series of tweens. The motionFinish event can be used to ensure calls to tween.yoyo() are only be made after the tween has stopped. Tween.yoyo causes the tween to play backwards to from its ending values back to its starting values.

Tween event object properties

Tween event objects all share some common properties.

event.target : The tween that dispatched the event.

event.time: The time of the tween when the event occurred.

event.position: The value of the property controlled by the tween, when the event occurred.

One very useful property of the tween event object is the event.target's obj property. The property event.target.obj gives a reference to the object controlled by the tween.

```
var tweenedObject:Object = event.target.obj;
```

Example – Tween events

File: [class files]/tweening/Example_tweenEvents.fla.

Overview

The example file demonstrates using tween events. The MOTION_FINISH event is used to call yoyo after a tween has finished playing.

Suggestions

1. Open and run the file. A figure moves from the left to the right of the screen and stops.
2. Examine the figure on stage. Notice that its registration point is in the center.
3. Examine the actions in frame 1 of the actions layer. Notice the compensation for the figure's width to keep the figure from appearing to go off stage.
4. Remove the comment from the line that assigns the handler for TweenEvent.MOTION_FINISH.
5. Run and test the file. Every time the tween finishes the event handler calls yoyo. This restarts the tween from the object's new position. Multiplying an object's scale by -1 is an old trick to 'flip' an object.
6. To have the runner stop after one 'round trip' remove the comment from the line that removes the listener for MOTION_FINISH.

Code – Tween events

```
import fl.transitions.*;
import fl.transitions.easing.*;
import flash.events.*;

// Variables.

// Set the runner on the left edge of the stage.
var startValue:Number = runner.width/2;

// Figure out where to stop the runner.
var finishValue:Number = stage.stageWidth -
runner.width/2;

// How many frames for the tween.
var duration:Number = 30;

// Initialize.
var tween:Tween = new Tween(runner, "x",
Strong.easeInOut, startValue, finishValue, duration);

// Handler assignment.
tween.addEventListener(TweenEvent.MOTION_FINISH,
doYoyo);


// Function.
function doYoyo(event:Event):void
{
   // Play tween in reverse.
   event.target.yoyo();
   event.target.obj.scaleX  *= -1;
   //
tween.removeEventListener(TweenEvent.MOTION_FINISH,
                                    doYoyo);
}
```

Applying tweens to the drag game

Related file: No file. This short discussion leads right into an exercise.

The drag game presents two places where programmatic tweens could be used effectively.

Instead of the game pieces jumping back to their starting place when they miss the target they could animate back.

The feedback at the end could be faded in instead of suddenly appearing.

Animating the game pieces

Animating the game pieces back to their starting position is fairly straight forward. It requires two tweens, one tween for the x movement and one for the y movement. The tweens will just use a lot of variables. The variables would include the object to tween, the starting positions and the ending positions.

The drag handler should be removed during tweening and reapplied when the motion has finished.

Triggering the feedback fade in

The feedback text should fade in when all three game pieces have been matched to their target. A variable could be created that holds the number of game pieces. This could be decremented until it reached 0. The feedback text would fade in when the counter reached 0.

Using a counting variable is not a bad solution. The only drawback is that if the number of game pieces changes the number assigned to the variable must be updated by the programmer.

A more elegant solution is to use the numChildren property. All movieClips have a property, numChildren, which gives the number of children they contain. This could be tested to see if it is 0.

An even more elegant solution would use the NOT operator (!) to see if there are not any children in the mcIcons

```
if (! mcIcons.numChildren )
{
   // Fade in feedback here.
}
```

Try it – Adding a tween to the drag game

Challenge

Use a tween to fade in the feedback movieClip at the end of the game. The tween can be written as a very simple one line declaration since it uses no variables.

There is a suggestion for solving the challenge on this page. A solution is offered following the challenge.

Extra challenging

Start with the drag game from the last chapter. Add tweens to make the game pieces return to their starting position if they are not put on target. No additional suggestions are provided. The solution is in the starter file for this challenge.

Starter File

[class files]/tweening/Begin_tweenDragGame.fla.

The starter file is based on the previous drag game example. The tweening to return the game pieces to their starting place has already been added.

The import statements for the Tween and Easing classes have been added.

An if statement is needed to see if mcIcons is empty. Inside the if a simple tween will be declared to fade mcFeedback in.

Suggestions

1. Open examine and run the file. Notice that the game pieces animate back to their starting positions. The feedback does not fade in.

2. Review the code. Examine the actions that have been added to tween the game pieces back to the starting positions. Notice that the drag handle is removed during tweening and reapplied when the tween is complete. Notice that mcFeedback's alpha is initially set to 0.

3. Find the comment that says:
   // Use a tween to fade mcFeedback in...
   // ...if mcIcons is empty.

4. After the comment, write an if statement that checks to see if mcIcons is empty.
5. In the if statement write a tween that change's mcFeedback's alpha property from 0 to 1.
6. Test.

SOLUTION – Using tweens

File: [class files]/tweening/Solution_tweenDragGame.fla.

```
// Required imports.
import fl.transitions.*;
import fl.transitions.easing.*;

// Declare two variables to hold...
// ...the game pieces starting position.
// These variables are needed in two functions so...
//  ...they must be declared outside of the functions.
var originalX:Number;
var originalY:Number;

// Variable to hold reference to selected clip.
var selectedClip:MovieClip;

// Initilization.
mcFeedback.alpha = 0;

// Show the finger when over game pieces.
mcIcons.buttonMode = true;

// Add properties to the game pieces.
// The properties will contain a reference...
// ... to the clips they should hit.
mcIcons.mcChicago.clipToHit = mcChicagoTarget;
mcIcons.mcNyc.clipToHit = mcNycTarget;
mcIcons.mcWdc.clipToHit = mcWdcTarget;

// Assign listeners to container holding game pieces.
mcIcons.addEventListener(MouseEvent.MOUSE_DOWN,
doDrag);
```

Code continues on the next page...

SOLUTION – Using tweens (continued)

```
// When a game piece is clicked on.
function doDrag(event:MouseEvent):void
{
   // Assign drop handler to stage.
   stage.addEventListener(MouseEvent.MOUSE_UP,
doDrop);
   // Create a variable for the selected...
   // ...object from the event target.
   // Cast it to a MovieClip.
   selectedClip = event.target as MovieClip;
   // Record the starting position.
   originalX = selectedClip.x;
   originalY = selectedClip.y;
   // Bring it to the front of its container.
   mcIcons.addChild(selectedClip);
   // Start dragging.
   selectedClip.startDrag();
}

// When a game piece is dropped.
function doDrop(event:MouseEvent):void
{
   // Remove listener from stage.
   stage.removeEventListener(MouseEvent.MOUSE_UP,
doDrop);
   // Create a variable for the clip to hit.
   var targetClip:MovieClip = selectedClip.clipToHit;

   // Stop dragging.
   selectedClip.stopDrag();
```

Code continues on the next page...

SOLUTION – Using tweens (continued)

```
   // See if the object was dropped on the correct
target.
   if ( selectedClip.hitTestObject( targetClip ) )
   {
         // Move selectedClip to the main timeline.
         addChild(selectedClip);
         // Bring the remaining icons...
         // ...to the front of everything.
         addChild(mcIcons);
         // Put the object on the target.
         selectedClip.x = targetClip.x;
         selectedClip.y = targetClip.y;

         // Use a tween to fade mcFeedback in...
         // ...if mcIcons is empty.
         if (! mcIcons.numChildren )
         {
              var tweenAlpha:Tween =
                 new Tween(mcFeedback, "alpha",
                       None.easeNone, 0, 1, 30);
         }
   }
   else
   {
         // Put the object back where it started.
         // Remove doDrag handler, prevent drag in
            tween.

   mcIcons.removeEventListener(MouseEvent.MOUSE_DOWN,
                                    doDrag);
         var duration:Number = 12;
         var startX:Number = event.target.x;
         var startY:Number = event.target.y;
         var finishX:Number = originalX;
         var finishY:Number = originalY;
```

Code continues on the next page...

SOLUTION – Using tweens

```
    var tweenX:Tween =
    new Tween(selectedClip, "x", Back.easeInOut,
              startX, finishX, duration);
    var tweenY:Tween =
     new Tween(selectedClip, "y", Back.easeInOut,
               startY, finishY, duration);
    tweenX.addEventListener(TweenEvent.MOTION_FINISH,
                            doMotionFinished);
    }
}

// When a game piece is dropped.
function doMotionFinished(event:TweenEvent):void
{
    // Add the doDrag handler to re-enable dragging.
    mcIcons.addEventListener(MouseEvent.MOUSE_DOWN,
    doDrag);
}
```

CHAPTER 8 - MOVIECLIPS AS BUTTONS

Overview

The SimpleButton class provides a fast, simple way to create highly interactive buttons but it has some important limitations. MovieClips can be easily turned into buttons with better functionality than simpleButtons.

It is fairly easy to turn a movieClip into a fully functioning button but the technique has received little publication.

This chapter shows how to use movieClips as buttons by themselves and in button groups.

Topics

- Advantages of MovieClips.
- Required frame labels
- Required ActionScript
- Increased functionality
- Storing extra information
- Button groups

Limitations of simpleButtons

The class used most commonly for buttons is called the SimpleButton class. It is easily identified by its unique fame labels. While simpleButtons are easy to use there are some important limitations to the SimpleButton class.

- It cannot easily show a disabled or off state.
- It cannot have new variables added to it.
- It cannot hold a label that can be set by ActionScript from outside.
- ActionScript inside a button does not work.

Extra state

The user experience can be improved by disabling a button if further clicking on it brings no new results. An example would be a button in a menu system that has loaded and displayed a file.

The button can indicate it has been selected by changing appearance and becoming inactive to the mouse. This can be done by adding an extra frame that holds the artwork for the disabled state. There is no easy way to do this using simpleButtons.

New variables

Adding new variables to a button can be very useful. It allows for much simpler event handling. These buttons can be grouped to provide navigation in the timeline or used to load external content.

Breaking a Flash application or Flash web site into multiple external files is a best practice as projects become larger and more complex. One master file then becomes a controller, loading and unloading content as needed.

Storing data in the buttons allows one handler to be used. In the event handler the extra data, such as the name of the file to load, can be extracted from the buttons. The event target provides an anonymous reference to whatever button was clicked. The extra data for the selected button can be gotten from event.target.

```
var fileToLoad:String = event.target.fileToLoad;
```

This technique will be used in many examples in this book.

Setting the button label with ActionScript

Being able to set a label in the button using ActionScript makes the button much more flexible. Multiple instances of one button can be used and their labels set via ActionScript.

Making a movieClip act like a button

Related file: The following file contains the examples for this discussion. [class files]/movieClipButtons/Example_movieClipButtons.fla.

Turning a movieClip into a button takes just a few steps. The frames of the simple button class must be recreated with frame labels. The label for the first frame is _up, the second frame label is _over, and the third frame label is _down. Those exact names must be used for those 3 frames.

The following is a list of the required labels for a movieClip button.

1. _up
2. _over
3. _down

Typically a separate layer is added to hold these frame labels.

Organizing artwork and frames in movieClip buttons is the same as it is for the simpleButtons. One or more key frames are used to hold artwork.

A few lines of ActionScript are needed in the first frame of the movieClip to finish turning it into a button.

A stop() action must be added to the first frame of the movie to keep the movie from playing automatically.

The movieClip's buttonMode should be set to true. This will turn the cursor into the hand icon when it is over the button.

Objects inside the movieClip need to be prevented from interfering with the mouse. Without this a text object inside a button would catch the mouse and prevent it from activating the button. This is prevented by setting the mouseChildren property to false.

Setting the trackAsMenu property to true is used to allow buttons to act as if they are in a group. When trackAsMenu is true, the users can do a mouse down on a button and hold the button down. While they are holding the mouse button down they can roll off the button they are on. As they roll over other buttons that have trackAsMenu set to true those buttons will activate. When trackAsMenu is set to false if the mouse goes down on a button and the mouse is held down and dragged over other buttons they will not respond to the mouse.

Finally, variables and possibly some functions are used inside the clip to set the button label and hold the extra data. This can be done with just variables but using a function to initialize the label and add the extra data is more flexible and robust. A function is needed to set the labels when the buttons are used in an advanced button group. A function will be used in this basic movieClip button example which will then be built into an advanced button group.

It is common to call functions to set the initial state of objects. The functions that initialize objects are often named init. This is a convention and not a requirement.

Actions inside the movieClip button

The following is an example of the typical actions in the first frame of a movieClip button.

```
// Hold the playback head here.
stop();

// Variable for extra data.
var extraInfo:String;
// Show the finger.
buttonMode = true;
// Stop mouse from interacting with...
// ...the label textField and other children.
mouseChildren = false;
// Allow mouse to move to and...
// ...activate other buttons while down.
trackAsMenu = true;

// Set the label and store extra data.
function init(btnLabel:String,
              argExtraInfo:String ):void
{
   label.text = btnLabel;
   extraInfo = argExtraInfo;
}
```

Preventing unwanted events

Just like simpleButtons, movieClips buttons can be gathered into another movieClip to simplify event handling. As usual, the movieClip that the buttons are in should be disabled from generating mouse actions. This prevents unwanted calls to the button group handlers.

```
// Prevent clicks in between buttons...
// ...in the buttonGroup from triggering handler.
buttonGroup.mouseEnabled = false;
```

This could be set from the main timeline. Eventually the button group container will carry a number of its own actions. In that case the best place for this ActionScript will be inside the container holding the buttons. This makes the statement even simpler.

```
// Prevent clicks in between buttons...
// ...in this movie clip from triggering handler.
mouseEnabled = false;
```

Configuring a button group

Assigning the button labels, extra information and handlers of a button group takes place in the parent of the button group. This will usually be the main timeline.

The following is an example of the typical actions used for configuring a button group.

```
// Initialize the buttons with labels and extra info.
buttonGroup.button1.init("Name 1","someData");
buttonGroup.button2.init("Name 2","someMoreData ");

// Assign handler.
buttonGroup.addEventListener(MouseEvent.MOUSE_UP,
                             clickHandler);

// Handler.
function clickHandler(event:Event):void
{
   // Retrieve the extra info from the buttons.
   trace(event.target.extraInfo);
}
```

Simpler updates

Updates to button groups using movieClip buttons are very easy. Simply add one or more new buttons to the group. Then initialize the buttons with their labels and extra data.

Example – Basic movieClip buttons

File:

[class files]/movieClipButtons/Example_movieClipButtons.fla.

Overview

The example file demonstrates how movieClips can function as buttons and hold extra information. In later examples the extra information will be the names of files to load.

Suggestions

1. Open and examine the file. MovieClip buttons have been collected into one movie clip on the stage. Examine the button container and the frame of the movieClip buttons.
2. Run the file. Click on the buttons. Observe the output of the traces.
3. Examine the actions in frame 1 of the actions layer.
4. The labels and the extra data are being applied to the movieClip buttons by calls to the init function inside each button. One handler is assigned to the button's container. The handler retrieves the extra data from each button.
5. Examine the code inside the buttonGroup movieClip. The only code there in this example prevents the group container from generating its own events. It does not affect the buttons.
6. Examine the code in frame 1 of the movieClip buttons.
    a. Comment out buttonMode = true Run the file and the hand icon does not appear when the button is rolled over. Remove the comment.
    b. Comment out mouseChildren = false. Run the file. Try to click on a button. The button does not work because the text object is capturing the mouse instead of the button. Remove the comment.

7. Explore trackAsMenu.
    a. Run the file. Click on a button and hold the mouse down. With the mouse held down drag the mouse over the other buttons. Notice that the buttons the mouse is dragged over activate.
    b. Comment out the line: trackAsMenu = true. Run the file. Click the mouse down on a button. Hold it down and drag it over the other buttons. The other buttons no longer activate. TrackAsMenu allows buttons to activate if the mouse is dragged from one button to another.

Code – Basic movieClip buttons

Code in frame 1 of actions layer in main timeline.

```
// Initialize the buttons with labels and extra info.
buttonGroup.button1.init("This","info");
buttonGroup.button2.init("That","more info");
buttonGroup.button3.init("A label","extra data");
buttonGroup.button4.init("Your msg here","someFile");

// Assign handler.
buttonGroup.addEventListener(MouseEvent.MOUSE_UP,
                             buttonGroupHandler);

// Handler.
function buttonGroupHandler(event:Event):void
{
   // Retrieve the extra info from the buttons.
   trace(event.target.extraData);
}
```

Code in frame 1 of buttonGroup.

```
// Prevent clicks in empty spaces of...
// ...buttonGroup from triggering handler.
buttonGroup.mouseEnabled = false;
```

Code continues on the next page...

Code – Basic movieClip buttons (continued)

Code in frame 1 of the movieClip button.

```
// Hold the playback head here.
stop();

// Variable for extra data.
var extraData:String;
// Show the finger.
buttonMode = true;
// Stop mouse from interacting with...
// ...textfield and other children.
mouseChildren = false;
// Allow mouse to move to and...
// ..activate other buttons while down.
trackAsMenu = true;

// Set the label and store extra data.
function init(btnLabel:String,
argExtraData:String):void
{
   label.text = btnLabel;
   extraData = argExtraData;
}
```

The hitArea

Related file: The following file contains the example for this discussion. [class files]/movieClipButtons/Example_hitArea.fla.

The movieClip button from the previous example works well but it could not be used in the automotive ad banner used in earlier examples.

That ad banner used simpleButtons that were hollow. The buttons were only an outline and had no artwork in the center. Because there was no artwork in the center the hit frame of the button was necessary. The artwork in the hit frame detected the mouse and made the button work.

MovieClip buttons do not use a special frame to define a hitArea. Instead a movieClip is used to hold the artwork that will detect the mouse. The movie clip can be given any name. The movieClip is positioned as needed to detect the mouse. The movieClip's instance name is applied as the hitArea property of the movieClip button. The movieClip for the hit area can be hidden by setting it's visible property to false. The hit area movieClip should have its mouseEnabled property set to false to keep it from interfering with the button's operation.

Steps to create the hit area in a movieClip button.

1. Create a movieClip that holds the artwork that will detect the mouse.
2. Place the new movieClip inside the movieClip button in its own layer. It only needs to be in the first frame.
3. Give the hit area clip an instance name. For this example the name mcHitArea was used.
4. In frame 1 of the actions layer in the movieClip button add the following ActionScript statements:
   - hitArea = mcHitArea;
   - mcHitArea.visible = false;
   - mcHitArea.mouseEnabled = false;

The hit area movieClip can have its alpha set and be given a tint so that it appears much the same way as Flash's simpleButton does.

Example – Hit Area

File: [class files]/movieClipButtons/Example_hitArea.fla.

Overview

The example file demonstrates how use a movieClip as the hit area for a movieClip button.

Suggestions

1. Open and run the file. Roll the mouse over the buttons.
2. The buttons work properly even though they are only outlines.
3. Examine the clipButton. Notice the extra movieClip inside named mcHitArea.
4. Examine the Actions in frame 1 of clipButton that refer to mcHitArea.

Code – Hit area

Code in frame 1 of actions layer in clipButton.

```
stop();
buttonMode = true;
hitArea = mcHitArea;
mcHitArea.visible = false;
mcHitArea.mouseEnabled = false;
```

Advanced movieClip button groups

Related file: The following file contains the example for this discussion. [class files]/movieClipButtons/Begin_movieClipButtons.fla.

Since movieClips are more versatile than simpleButtons they can be given advanced interactivity. They can change appearance to indicate that they are the button that is selected. This creates a button group that functions in the same fashion as a radio button group. Only one button can be selected at a time. The selected button shows that it is selected by changing appearance. The selected button is disabled from being selected again until a different button is selected.

To create this functionality some code is changed in the button, more actions are added to the container clip and the button handler needs an extra action.

Changes in movieClip button

An additional action is added to frame 1. A new frame and frame label are added at the end of the timeline. The new frame will contain additional actions and the artwork for the disabled state.

The button will be disabled by sending its playback head to the new frame. It will be re-enabled by sending its playback head to frame 1.

Additional action in frame 1 of movieClip button

One additional action has to be added to the first frame of the movieClip button. Eventually the button will be disabled by setting mouseEnabled to false and sending the playback head to a new frame with artwork for the disabled state. One extra action in the first frame will re-enable the movieClip when the playback head is sent to back frame 1, the _up frame.

```
// This re-enables the button after...
// ...it has been sent to the _off frame.
mouseEnabled = true;
```

Extra frame for the disabled state

An extra frame is added to the movieClip button to hold the artwork and actions for the disabled state. There is no built in key word for the label for the disabled frame. The extra frame label can use any name.

The frame label _off is used in this course. There is no technical requirement to use an underscore with this frame's label. The underscore is used to be consistent with the other labels of this type.

Actions are added to the _off frame of the button clip to disable the clip when the playback head is sent there.

```
// Make the button inactive.
buttonMode = false;
mouseEnabled = false;
mouseChildren = false;
```

Changes to container clip

The movieClip buttons are collected in a container clip just as they were in other examples. This container movieClip is the best place to hold the extra actions for the logic that disables and re-enables the buttons.

Extra actions in the container clip

The following are the typical actions used in frame 1 of the container clip holding the advanced movieClip buttons.

These actions disable the button the user selects and re-enables the last button that was disabled. The code uses an if statement to keep from throwing an error the first time a button is selected. The if statement will only try to use the variable disabledButton if disabledButton has been assigned a value.

Typical actions used in frame 1 of the button container clip:

```
// Create a variable to remember which button was
disabled.
var disabledButton:MovieClip;

// Prevent clicks in between buttons...
// ...in this clip from triggering handler.
mouseEnabled = false;

// Re-enable the disabled button.
// Disable button just selected.
// Called from main timeline.
function setButtons(selectedButton:MovieClip):void
{
   // If prevents errors the first time...
   // ...setButtons is called when...
   // ...there is no disabledButton.
   if (disabledButton)
   {
        // Enable old button.
        disabledButton.gotoAndStop("_up");
   }
   // Disable the selected button.
   selectedButton.gotoAndStop("_off");
   // Store which button is now disabled.
   disabledButton = selectedButton;
}
```

Changes to main timeline

In the main timeline the handler assignment and the initialization of the buttons stay the same. The buttonGroupHandler is changed.

The buttonGroupHandler needs to call setButtons inside the buttonGroup movieClip every time a button is selected. SetButtons needs to be passed the selected button. This can be done by passing event.target.

```
buttonGroup.setButtons(event.target);
```

This call will disable and enable the appropriate buttons in the buttonGroup as buttons are selected.

Setting an initial button as selected

Trying to set the initial button to be selected by simply calling buttonGroupHandler directly presents a problem. ButtonGroupHandler requires an event object as its argument. If the buttonGroupHandler is called directly the call would have to pass a custom event object as its argument. The creation of custom event objects is beyond the scope of this course. It is covered in the advanced ActionScript courses.

Instead of calling the buttonGroupHandler, the setButtons() method is called inside the buttonGroup. The instance name of the button to be selected is passed to setButtons().

In addition, any actions that would have been run by selecting the button need to be executed manually.

The following example shows the selection of the initial button.

```
// Following simulates selection of initial button.
// Set the first button.
buttonGroup.setButtons(buttonGroup.button1);

// Do whatever selecting the initial button would do.
trace(buttonGroup.button1.extraInfo);

// Assign handler.
buttonGroup.addEventListener(MouseEvent.MOUSE_UP,
                             buttonGroupHandler);

// Handler.
function buttonGroupHandler(event:Event):void
{
   // Toggle the buttons.
   buttonGroup.setButtons(event.target as MovieClip);
   // Use the extra info from the selected button.
   trace(event.target.extraInfo);
}
```

Try it – Advanced movieClip buttons

Challenge

Use an advanced button group.

Initialize the group by setting the buttons' labels and extra data. Select the initial button.

This file will be the basis for an example in the next chapter.

There is a suggestion for solving the challenge on this page. A solution is offered following the challenge.

Starter File

[class files]/movieClipButtons/Begin_advMcButtons.fla.

The starter file is based on the previous movieClip button example. The extra code and frames needed to turn it into an advanced button group have been added.

Suggestions

7. Review the extra code that has been added to the button group.
8. Examine the extra frame in the movieClip button. Examine the code in the first and last frame of the movieClip button.
9. Initialize the three buttons from the main timeline. Their extra data will be the names of files that will be loaded in the next chapter. Use the following labels and extra data. Use the following labels and filenames. This information is also in comments inside the starter file.
   - Times Square - timesSquare.jpg
   - Chicago - navyPier.jpg
   - Jackson Square - JacksonSquare.jpg
10. Add the two calls to setButtons that are needed. One is used to set the first button. The other is used inside the button group handler to change the selected button.
11. Test.

SOLUTION – Advanced movieClip buttons

File: [class files]/movieClipButtons/Solution_advMcButtons.fla

This file provides a solution for the challenge.

Frame 1 of actions layer in the main timeline.

```
// Initialize the buttons with labels and extra info.
buttonGroup.button1.initBtn("Times Square",
                            "timesSquare.jpg");
buttonGroup.button2.initBtn("Chicago","navyPier.jpg");
buttonGroup.button3.initBtn("Jackson Square",
                            "jacksonSquare.jpg");

// Following simulates selection of initial button.
// Set the first button.
buttonGroup.setButtons(buttonGroup.button1);
// Do whatever selecting the initial button would do.
trace(buttonGroup.button1.extraData);

// Assign handler.
buttonGroup.addEventListener(MouseEvent.MOUSE_UP,
                             buttonGroupHandler);

// Handler.
function buttonGroupHandler(event:Event):void
{
   // Toggle the buttons.
   buttonGroup.setButtons(event.target as MovieClip);
   // Use the extra info from the selected button.
   trace(event.target.extraData);
}
```

CHAPTER 9 – LOADING CONTENT

Overview

Flash applications can load and display several types of external media. There are many ways that external media can be useful to developers and end users. Creating an application that uses external content is the best way to architect larger projects.

Topics

- Benefits of external content
- Opening a web page or file
- Security issues
- Components
- Loading text and HTML
- Styling text and HTML
- Loading images
- Progress bars/preloaders

External content

Developers need to make decisions about which content should be included in the SWF and which content should be kept externally and loaded as it is needed.

Including content directly in a SWF ensures the content is quickly available when needed, once the SWF is loaded. The amount of time that it takes to load a larger SWF becomes a problem. A SWF with all internal content will take longer to load and take longer before the user to interact with it.

As the amount of content in a Flash project increases a point will be reached where the initial loading will take too long. Large SWFs may not provide a good user experience even over high bandwidth connections.

In such content heavy Flash applications the application can be broken into separate parts containing different content. These individual parts are often other SWFs. These SWFs can have their content embedded or they too can load other external content such as text and graphics.

In addition to improving download and startup times using external content can make updates and other maintenance easier. Images, text, HTML and SWFs stored externally can be changed without the need to recompile the main SWF. Breaking content into separate files also allows for simultaneous development by teams.

Content that can be kept separate and loaded into SWFs includes other SWFs, graphics, text and some HTML. Those content types are the focus of this chapter. Audio and video can also be kept as external files. Those content types are covered in the Advanced ActionScript course.

Web pages and other file types

Related file: The following file contains the examples for this discussion. [class files]/loadingContent/Example_navigateToUrl.fla.

Web pages and other file types are a special case of external content. While Flash has some ability to render HTML it is very limited and comparable to HTML 1.0. Using HTML inside of Flash is covered later in this chapter. Most web pages will be too complex for Flash to render and must be loaded into a browser on their own.

Developers can link to and load complex external web pages from their Flash applications. This technique can also be used to link to other types of files. The web pages will open in a browser. Other types of files will open in the browser or open a window to allow downloading the file.

To open a web page in a browser, or download a file, an URLRequest object must be created and passed as an argument to a navigateToURL method.

The URLRequest object can be created with the absolute or relative path to the desired web page or file. When making a request to an absolute address outside of the host domain the full address including the protocol should be used.

For example, http://www.adobe.com/ should be used instead of just adobe.com.

The URLRequest object can be built using two lines.

```
var urlToGoTo:String = "http://www.adobe.com/";
var urlRequest:URLRequest = new URLRequest(urlToGoTo);
```

This can be useful if more than one web page will be opened. Creating a variable allows the same URLRequest object to be reused. The value of the urlToGoTo variable can simply be changed and a new URLRequest object with the same name and the new argument created.

If only one web page is to be loaded a little memory can be saved by combining the two lines into one.

```
var urlRequest:URLRequest =
   new URLRequest("http://www.adobe.com/");
```

The URLRequest object is then used as an argument to the navigateToURL method.

```
navigateToURL( urlRequest );
```

The entire process can be reduced to one line if desired.

```
navigateToURL(new
URLRequest("http://www.adobe.com/"));
```

If the SWF is running in the desktop player a web browser will open and attempt to open the page or file requested. If the SWF is running in a web browser the request will open in a new tab or new browser window and attempt to load the request.

To open the new page in the same tab or browser window a second argument can be added to the navigateToURL method. The second argument specifies the window to use.

```
navigateToURL( urlRequest, "_self");
```

When the second argument is "_self" it causes the requested page to open in the same tab or web browser window as the SWF that made the request.

Example – navigateToURL

File: [class files]/loadingContent/Example_navigateToUrl.fla.

Overview

The example file demonstrates opening a web page. The same technique can be used to link to a file. A button calls a handler. The handler builds an URLRequest and uses it in a call to navigateToURL.

Suggestions

1. Open and run the file. Press the button over the company name in the left side of the banner. A browser opens and loads a web page.
2. Examine the actions in frame 1 of the actions layer.
3. Change the code to open a different web page.
4. Launch the file in a browser and test.
   To launch in a browser:
   - File > Publish Preview > HTML
   - ...or on many systems; Press the F12 key.
5. Add a second argument to naviagteToURL to open the page in a new tab or browser.
6. Test the changes.

Code – navigateToURL

Frame 1 of actions layer in the main timeline

Simplified

```
btnLink.addEventListener("click", openLink);

function openLink(event:Event):void
{
   navigateToURL(new
URLRequest("http://jalopnik.com"));
}
```

Lengthy but potentially more versatile

```
var urlToGoTo:String = "http://jalopnik.com/";

var urlRequest:URLRequest = new URLRequest(urlToGoTo);

btnLink.addEventListener("click", openLink);

function openLink(event:Event):void
{
   navigateToURL( urlRequest );
}
```

About security

When navigateToURL is used the actual task of handling the request is passed off to a browser. Any request that can be handled outside of the Flash player and directly by in the browser can be made by using navigateToURL. Loading content directly into the Flash player is more restricted.

Generally speaking, content cannot be loaded directly into the Flash player unless it comes from the same domain as the SWF requesting it.

Requests for content from another domain can work if a cross-domain policy file is in place in the other domain. A cross-domain policy file is an XML document that grants the Flash Player permission to load content from that domain.

The cross-domain policy file specification and other information is available from Adobe.

http://learn.adobe.com/wiki/download/attachments/64389123/CrossDomain_PolicyFile_Specification.pdf

About components

Related file: The following file contains the examples for this discussion. [class files]/loadingContent/Example_loadImages.fla.

Components are a special type of MovieClip. Components are wrappers placed around ActionScript classes. These wrappers are intended to make the classes easier to use. These wrappers provide classes that might otherwise be intangible with a physical presence on the stage. The artwork in visible components can be changed by going into the Component, just like going into a MovieClip and changing the artwork.

Components can be configured by setting their properties in the Component section of the Properties panel (the Component Inspector in older versions) or by using ActionScript.

In very small, simple applications the Component section of the Properties panel provides a fast and easy way to configure components. However there is no way to tell by looking at the code if properties have been set this way. Larger, more complex applications should use ActionScript to configure the components instead of the Properties panel.

This provides documentation in the code about which properties have been set and what their values are.

All examples in this course configure components using ActionScript.

Loading graphics into a component

Graphics in the formats commonly used for web pages can be easily loaded into Flash at runtime. The component for doing this is the UILoader. This is a wrapper around the Loader class. The UILoader component is a wrapper for the Loader class.

The following is a list of supported formats supported by the Loader class and the UILoader component.

- SWF
- GIF
- JPEG
- PNG

Graphics can be loaded into the UILoader using either the source property or the load() method.

Using the load() method requires creating an URLRequest object and using it as the argument to load().

```
uiLoader.load(new URLRequest( "somefile.xyz");
```

The source property is slightly easier to use. The UILoader source property takes a simple string representing the location of the file.

```
uiLoader.source = "someDirectory/somefile.xyz";
```

The source property will be used in the examples in this chapter.

Here are some important UILoader properties.

- **autoLoad:** Default value is true.
  When autoLoad is set to true it causes the UILoader to automatically load content whenever the value of the source property is assigned a value.

- **scaleContent:** Default value is true.
  Indicates whether the image being loaded is automatically sized to the size of the UILoader instance.
- **maintainAspectRatio:** Default value is true.
  Indicates whether to maintain the aspect ratio that was used in the original image or to resize the image at the current width and height of the UILoader component.

If the images being loaded are the same width and height as the UILoader these properties can be kept at their defaults.

Scaling issue

There is a known problem with scaling and the UILoader component.

Sometimes when content is loaded it is not scaled properly. This can even happen when a 1:1 relationship has been created between the source content and the UILoader's size.

The solution is simple. Set the UILoader's scaleContent property to false.

```
uiLoader.scaleContent = false;
```

An example of the scaling issue in action is included with the class files. The directory [class files]/loadingContent/scalingIssue contains both FLAs and SWFs.

The name of the UILoader is contentLoader.

Running Example_ScalingIssueLoader.fla or Example_ScalingIssueLoader.swf and clicking on the buttons will show the problem.

The problem can be fixed by setting contentLoader's scaleContent property to false.

```
contentLoader.scaleContent = false;
```

Example – Loading images

File: [class files]/loadingContent/Example_loadImages.fla.

Overview

The example file demonstrates loading images into a UILoader component.

A UILoader has been placed on the stage. It is the same size as the images that will be loaded. This assists in positioning it on the stage..

This file is based on the advanced movieClip button file from the previous chapter. The name of the file that each button should load is stored in the extraData properties in buttons. The button handler uses the extraData property from the selected button to load the image.

There is no _down frame. The user would never see it because the button handler, buttonGroupHandler, is set to respond to MOUSE_OVER events. As soon as the mouse rolls over a button that button is disabled and sent to the _off frame. Since it is not needed the _down frame has been removed. The same artwork is used in both the _over and _down frames.

The images used in this example are stored in a directory named images in the directory [class files]/loadingContent/. The images directory needs to be in the same directory as the example file unless the path is edited in the button handler.

Suggestions

1. Open and run the file. Roll the mouse over the buttons. A different image is loaded as each button is rolled over.
2. Examine the actions in frame 1 of the actions layer.
3. This file uses the same code as the advanced movieClip button file from the previous chapter.
4. The buttonGroupHandler is called by MOUSE_OVER events.
5. The buttons have been initialized with their labels and the name of the files they should load.

6. In the buttonGroupHandler the name of the file to load is concatenated with the path to the directory holding the images. This is assigned to the uiLoader's source property.
7. The default value for a uiLoader's autoLoad property is true. Setting the source causes the file to load.

Code – Loading images

Frame 1 of actions layer in the main timeline

```
// Initialize the buttons with labels and extra info.
buttonGroup.button1.initBtn("Times Square",
                            "timesSquare.jpg");
buttonGroup.button2.initBtn("Chicago","navyPier.jpg");
buttonGroup.button3.initBtn("Jackson Square",
                            "jacksonSquare.jpg");

// Set the first button.
buttonGroup.setButtons(buttonGroup.button1);
// Load the first image.
uiLoader.source = "images/timesSquare.jpg";

// Assign handler.
buttonGroup.addEventListener(MouseEvent.MOUSE_OVER,
                             buttonGroupHandler );

// Handlers.
function completeHandler (event:Event):void
{
   event.target.visible = false;
}

function buttonGroupHandler (event:Event):void
{
   // Variable to hold a reference to the selected
button.
   var selectedButton:MovieClip =
       event.target as MovieClip;
   // Toggle the buttons.
   buttonGroup.setButtons(selectedButton);
   // Build the name and path for the file to load.
   var fileToLoad = "images/" +
selectedButton.extraInfo;
   // Load the file.
   uiLoader.source = fileToLoad;
}
```

ProgressBar

Related file: The following file contains the examples for this discussion. [class files]/loadingContent/Example_progressBar.fla.

A ProgressBar component can be used to give users feedback about the status of images being loaded. A ProgressBar can easily be used with the UILoader.

A ProgressBar will display the loading status of any UILoader that is assigned to the ProgressBar's source property.

```
progressBar.source = uiLoader;
```

The ProgressBar usually needs to be hidden after the content has been loaded. The ProgressBar (and the uiLoader) will generate a COMPLETE event when the loading is finished. A handler for the COMPLETE event can be used to hide the ProgressBar.

```
progressBar.addEventListener(Event.COMPLETE,
                                   completeHandler);

function completeHandler(event:Event):void
{
   event.target.visible = false;
}
```

The ProgressBar can be made visible again the next time the handler that loads the content is called.

The Loader class, and the UILoader component that encapsulates it, generate events that contain information about the progress of the loading operation. These events can be used to create custom feedback and control custom progress bars. This is covered in the Advanced ActionScript course.

This class uses the ProgressBar component instead of a custom pre-loader solution.

Simulating a download

Developers can see how their project will load at different bandwidths. When the Test Movie command is used to preview a project menu items become available that will simulate a download. These menu items are not available in the main Flash interface. They are only available in the window that opens while running Test Movie in Flash.

In the View menu when running Test Movie there is a selection labeled Download Settings. From the Download Settings a bandwidth can be selected. By choosing Simulate Download from the same View menu the movie will be played the way a user would see it load at the selected bandwidth.

Example – Progress bar

File: [class files]/loadingContent/Example_progressBar.fla.

Overview

The example file demonstrates using a ProgressBar and UILoader component. The ProgressBar is set to use information from the UILoader. Handlers are used to show and hide the ProgressBar as needed.

One new handler and three new lines of code are added to the previous example.

The file will need to be run in Simulate Download mode to see the ProgressBar work.

Suggestions

1. Open and run the file.
2. Select a download speed from the Download Settings.
3. Run the file using Simulate Download.
    - A ProgressBar component provides feedback about the loading.
    - The ProgressBar disappears when the image is completely loaded.
    - It reappears when the next image is called for.
4. Examine the code in frame 1 of the main timeline.
5. The uiLoader is assigned as the source property of the progress bar.
6. A hander is assigned to the progressBar COMPLETE event.
7. The COMPLETE event handler sets the visible property of the ProgressBar to false hiding it.
8. The buttonGroupHandler sets the visible property of the ProgressBar to true, showing the ProgressBar when the next image is loaded.

9. Notice that the ProgressBar reappears and the image appears to reload. This occurs because the download simulator does not emulate a browser's caching capabilities. When the SWF is run in a browser from a web server each image should be cached and should show the progress bar only once.

Code – Progress bar

```
// Initialize progressBar.
// Set component progressBar should monitor.
progressBar.source = uiLoader;

// Initialize the buttons with labels and extra info.
buttonGroup.button1.initBtn("New
York","timesSquare.jpg");
buttonGroup.button2.initBtn("Chicago","navyPier.jpg");
buttonGroup.button3.initBtn("San Francisco",
                              "jacksonSquare.jpg");

// Set the first button.
buttonGroup.setButtons(buttonGroup.button1);
// Load the first image.
uiLoader.source = "images/timesSquare.jpg";

// Assign handlers.
// Assign handler to hide progressBar when finished.
progressBar.addEventListener(Event.COMPLETE,
                              completeHandler);

buttonGroup.addEventListener(MouseEvent.MOUSE_OVER,
                              buttonGroupHandler);

// Handlers.
function completeHandler(event:Event):void
{
   event.target.visible = false;
}
```

Code continues on next page...

Code – Progress bar (continued)

```
function buttonGroupHandler(event:Event):void
{
   // Show progressBar.
   progressBar.visible = true;
   // Variable to hold a reference
   // to the selected button.
   var selectedButton:MovieClip
     =event.target as MovieClip;
   // Toggle the buttons.
   buttonGroup.setButtons(selectedButton);
   // Build the name and path for the file to load.
   var fileToLoad = "images/" +
selectedButton.extraInfo;
   // Load the file.
   uiLoader.source = fileToLoad;
}
```

Loading text

Related file: The following file contains the examples for this discussion. [class files]/loadingContent/Example_loadText.fla.

Text can be loaded into Flash at runtime. The text can be in the form of plain text or marked up with HTML. There are no prebuilt components for loading text. Loading text is accomplished entirely in ActionScript using the URLLoader class.

Text can be displayed in TextField objects. In addition to the TextField objects there is a ScrollBar component, a TextArea component and a Label component that are useful for displaying text.

Loading text is only slightly different from loading images. When loading an image a request is made for the image. After a delay the image is completely loaded and then automatically appears in the UILoader. Loaded text requires specific actions to make the text appear to the user after it is loaded.

A call for text is made using an URLRequest object and an instance of the URLLoader class. The text cannot be used until it has finished loading. The URLLoader will generate a COMPLETE event when the text has completely finished loading. The COMPLETE handler is the place to do things with the freshly loaded text. The text will be in the data property of the URLLoader. The URLLoader can be referenced as the target property of the COMPLETE event.

The following is an example of loading and displaying text.

```
var urlRequest:URLRequest =
    new URLRequest("someDirectory/someText.txt");

var urlLoader:URLLoader = new URLLoader(urlRequest);

urlLoader.addEventListener(Event.COMPLETE,
onComplete);

function onComplete(event:Event):void
{
   someTextField.text = event.target.data;
}
```

Instantiating the new URLLoader with an URLRequest object will cause the text to be loaded.

Removing extra carriage returns

Text will often appear in TextFields with more new lines/carriage returns than expected. This has to do with some text editors and the Windows OS adding hidden characters for both line feeds and carriage returns when the enter key is pressed to add a new line. Text objects in Flash process and use both of those hidden characters creating the extra lines. Those extra lines of white space can be removed with a bit of extra code.

```
myTextField.text =
event.target.data.split("\n").join("");
```

This extra code splits the text into separate elements wherever the hidden characters for a new line character are found (\n) and discards the new line character. It then joins the split elements back together without adding anything between the concatenated parts ("").

TextField properties

The following TextField properties need to be set to enable word wrapping and multiple lines of text. These can be set using the Properties Panel or with ActionScript.

```
txtContent.multiline = true;
txtContent.wordWrap = true;
```

Styling TextField objects

TextField objects have a number of properties that can change their appearance. Many of these properties are not available through the property inspector.

The following is an example of how to turn the background and border on in a textField object and set their color using ActionScript.

```
someTextField.background = true;
someTextField.backgroundColor = 0xCCCCCC;
someTextField.border = true;
someTextField.borderColor = 0xFF0000;
```

The 0x in front of the Hexadecimal number converts the Hexadecimal number to the base 10 number Flash wants.

Styling text

Plain text in TextField objects can be styled by creating TextFormat objects and applying them to the text field. HTML formatted text uses CSS for styling.

The following example sets the font face, color and size.

```
var textFormat:TextFormat = new TextFormat();
textFormat.font = "Verdana";
textFormat.color = 0x000033;
textFormat.size = 16;
someTextField.defaultTextFormat = textFormat;
```

Applying the TextFormat object to the defaultTextFormat property ensures that the formatting will apply even when the text is changed and updated.

Fonts and text objects

For fonts to work properly in text objects the information to correctly render the fonts must be embedded in the SWF. Embedding fonts will add to the SWF's file size. Without embedding fonts will not display in the correct face, appear aliased (jagged), disappear when rotated and not be affected by alpha/transparency.

The following technique will embed fonts in Flash CS5 and earlier versions.

With the FLA file open in Flash, open the Font Embedding dialog box selecting any text object and using the Embed button in the Properties panel.

Select the font you want to embed in the list on the left.

In the options panel on the right select the characters you want to embed. Not all characters have to be embedded. For example, if the application only needs to display a score only the numerical characters would need to be embedded. Generally the Basic Latin set will be the best choice for an inclusive font set.

UIScrollBars and TextFields

When text is too lengthy to fit completely in a text object a scroll bar is needed. Scroll bars are built into the TextArea component. A ScrollBar component can be added to TextFields.

A component called the UIScrollBar can be added to TextField objects. After adding a UIScrollBar to a project and adjusting its size and position it must be associated with the TextField it needs to control. This can be done using the scrollTargetName parameter in the Component Inspector. This value can also be set with ActionScript. The property name in ActionScript is different from the parameter name in the Component Inspector. When using ActionScript the property name is simply scrollTarget.

The best practice will be to set the UIScrollBar's scrollTarget propert using ActionScript.

```
scrollBar.scrollTarget = someTextField;
```

There is a small trick that can make positioning and sizing the Scrollbar easier. Put the ScrollBar in the same layer as the TextField. Drop the ScrollBar directly on the TextField it will be associated with and it will automatically size itself and attach itself into position. Be sure the point of the cursor is over the TextField on the side the ScrollBar should attach to.

Dropping the UIScrollBar on the TextField will also set the scrollTargetName property in the Component Inspector. The best practice will be to set the UIScrollBar's scrollTarget property again using ActionScript.

Whenever the text changes in the TextField controlled by the UIScrollBar the update method of the UIScrollBar must be called. This causes the UIScrollBar to adjust itself to the new content.

```
scrollBar.update();
```

If the text is too short to need a scroll bar the UIScrollBar will still be visible. There is no simple, convenient way to know that the text is short, hide the scroll bar and make the TextField wider. The TextArea component has those capabilities built in. The only downside to using a TextArea component is that the TextArea component does not support CSS.

Example – Loading text

File: [class files]/loadingContent/Example_loadText.fla

Overview

This example loads simple text and displays it in a TextField on the stage. A TextArea will be used with HTML formatted text in the next example.

A UIScrollBar has not been added to the TextField. It will be added as part of the example.

The text file used in this example is stored in a directory named text inside the [class files]/loadingContent/ directory. The text directory needs to be in the same directory as the example file unless the path is edited in the onComplete handler.

Suggestions

1. Open and run the file. Text appears in a TextField named txtContent on the stage. Notice the extra empty lines between paragraphs.
2. Examine the actions in frame 1 of the actions layer.
    - The first two sections configure and style txtContent.
    - The third section creates a TextFormat object to style the text and applies it to the defaultTextFormat property of txtContent.
    - The onComplete handler assigns the loaded text to the text property of onComplete.
3. Modify the code to remove the extra line breaks.
4. Change the line assigning the text from:
   txtContent.text = event.target.data to:
   txtContent.text = event.target.data.split("\n").join("");
   Do this by either editing the line or deleting the current line and removing the comment from the next line.
5. Run the file again. The extra empty lines should be gone.

6. Add a UIScrollBar to the TextField.
    - Open the Components window.
    - Drag a UIScrollBar component from the Components window.
    - Drop it on the txtContent TextField when the mouse is over the left edge of the TextField. The scroll bar will dock to the right edge of the TextField and size itself to fit. (If it does not dock and size itself, drag and drop it on the TextField again. Be sure the mouse is over the TextField.)
7. Give the UIScrollBar an instance name of scrollBar.
8. Modify the code in frame 1 of the actions layer.
    - Remove the comment from the first line of code.
      scrollBar.scrollTarget = txtContent;
      This associates the scroll bar with the text field.
    - In the onCompleteHandler notice the line:
      ```
      scrollBar.update();
      ```
      This would cause the scroll bar to adjust to the proper length when the length of the text changes. This line is not necessary for this example to work properly but would be needed if new text was assigned after the initial load.
9. Run the file and test the scroll bar.

Code – Loading text

```
scrollBar.scrollTarget = txtContent;

// 1 Configure txtContent.
txtContent.multiline = true;
txtContent.wordWrap = true;

// 2 Style txtContent.
txtContent.background = true;
txtContent.backgroundColor = 0xEEEEFF;
txtContent.border = true;
txtContent.borderColor = 0x000099;

// 3 Format the text that will be rendered in
txtContent.
var textFormat:TextFormat = new TextFormat();
textFormat.font = "Verdana";
textFormat.color = 0x000033;
textFormat.size = 16;
txtContent.defaultTextFormat = textFormat;

// 4 Load the text.
var urlRequest:URLRequest =
    new URLRequest("text/timesSquare.txt");
var urlLoader:URLLoader = new URLLoader(urlRequest);
urlLoader.addEventListener(Event.COMPLETE,
onComplete);

// Handle the text when it is finished loading.
function onComplete(event:Event):void
{
   txtContent.text=event.target.data.split("\n").join(
"");
   // The next line is not needed in this example.
   // Needed if new text of different length is
assigned.
   // scrollBar.update();
}
```

HTML formatted text

Related files: The following files contain the examples for this discussion.
[class files]/loadingContent/Example_loadHTML.fla
[class files]/loadingContent/Example_externalCss.fla
[class files]/loadingContent/timesSquare.html
[class files]/loadingContent/css/styles.css

HTML can be used to provide rich, formatted text. To use HTML formatted text the text must be applied to the htmlText property of text objects.

```
myTextField.htmlText = event.target.data;
```

Text objects in Flash only support a very small set of HTML. The following is a list of the tags natively supported. Additional HTML tags can be rendered by the use of style objects or style sheets.

The following is a list of supported HTML tags.

- Anchor <a>
  The anchor tag has no default decoration. (i.e. blue and underlined.) Styles must be used to decorate links.
- Bold <b>
- Break
- Font <font>
- Image <img>
- Italic <i>
- List Item <li>
  Flash only renders unordered lists. <ol> and <ul> are treated the same.
- Paragraph <p>
- Underline <u>

Relative paths

Be careful when using relative paths in HTML files loaded into SWFs. The path will be resolved relative to the location of the SWF, not the

HTML file. This can create problems with links, images and other tags that reference relative paths.

Locating HTML files in the same directory as the SWF that loads them eliminates these issues.

Cascading Style Sheets

HTML formatted text can be styled using CSS. The CSS cannot be declared or linked to inside the HTML document as would normally be done. The CSS must be applied to the text object inside of the FLA.

If a style sheet is applied to a text object, even if it is set to allow text input, the text field will not accept user input.

The CSS can be kept in the FLA or in an external file. CSS kept in external files uses standard CSS syntax. CSS declarations in ActionScript are only slightly different from standard CSS.

CSS in ActionScript

To create CSS in ActionScript objects are created holding properties and values. These objects are then assigned to styles in a StyleSheet object. This assignment is done using the setStyle method of the StyleSheet class. The StyleSheet object is then applied to the styleSheet property of the TextField.

The following example shows how to create and apply a style for the h1 tag.

```
var styleSheet:StyleSheet = new StyleSheet();

var h1:Object = new Object();
h1.fontWeight = "bold";
h1.color = "#6666CC";
h1.fontSize = 20;

styleSheet.setStyle("h1", h1);

txtContent.styleSheet = styleSheet;
```

The objects holding the styling properties and values can be given any name. They are mapped to the appropriate style in the setStyle method.

For convenience the objects are usually given a name similar to, or identical to, the style they will be applied to.

Object literals

The syntax for creating styling objects can be simplified. Instead of assigning a value to each property in separate statements all of the properties can be set when the object is first created. This is done by using an abbreviated syntax that creates what are called object literals. These objects are still applied to the StyleSheet using setStyle just as in the previous example.

```
var h2:Object = { fontWeight:"bold",
                  color:"#666CC",
                  fontSize:18
                }
```

This syntax is very similar to the standard syntax for CSS.

External CSS

CSS declarations can be kept in external files and loaded at run time. This allows the CSS to be changed without needing to recompile the SWF. The CSS used in external files follows standard CSS syntax rules.

Loading external CSS files is handled the same as any other text file. An URLRequest is passed to an URLLoader. After the loading is complete the raw data is converted for use in the StyleSheet using the parseCSS method of the StyleSheet class. The StyleSheet is then applied to the TextField as usual.

```
var sheet:StyleSheet = new StyleSheet();

var cssRequest:URLRequest =
        new URLRequest("css/styles.css");

var cssLoader:URLLoader = new URLLoader();

cssLoader.addEventListener(Event.COMPLETE,
                              cssLoadedHandler);

cssLoader.load(cssRequest);

function cssLoadedHandler(event:Event):void
{
   sheet.parseCSS(event.target.data);
   txtContent.styleSheet = sheet;
}
```

Examples – HTML and CSS

Flash files:

[class files]/loadingContent/Example_loadHTML.fla
[class files]/loadingContent/Example_externalCss.fla

HTML file:

[class files]/loadingContent/timesSquare.html

CSS file:

[class files]/loadingContent/css/styles.css

Overview

There are two sets of examples. The example files demonstrate loading and styling HTML. One example uses style objects created using ActionScript. The other example uses styles from an external style sheet.

Suggestions

First Example - Using style objects

1. Open and run Example_loadHTML.fla. The SWF opens and displays HTML formatted text styled with ActionScript style objects.
2. Examine the actions in frame 1 of the actions layer in the main timeline.
   - Loading HTML is handled the same as loading text.
   - The data from the result object is applied to the htmlText property instead of the text property.
3. Examine the body and h1 style objects. Notice that they are created by instantiating an object and then populating the objects properties.
4. Examine the other style declarations. Notice that they are created and populated in one expression using object literal syntax.
5. Examine the lines that use the setStyle method of the StyleSheet class.
   - The first argument is in quotes. It is the literal name of the HTML element that the style object will be applied to.

- The second argument is the style object that will be applied to the HTML element.
- Once the styles are set in the StyleSheet object the StyleSheet object is applied to the text object's styleSheet property.

Second Example - Using an external style sheet

1. Open and run Example_externalCss.fla. The SWF opens and displays HTML formatted text styled with an external style sheet.
2. Examine the actions in frame 1 of the actions layer in the main timeline.
   - There are no style objects in this example.
   - External style sheets are loaded in the same fashion as any other text file.
   - Once the external style sheet has been loaded the parseCSS method of the StyleSheet class is used to populate a StyleSheet object.
   - The StyleSheet object is then applied to the StyleSheet property of the text object.

Code – Example_loadHTML.fla

```
var styleSheet:StyleSheet = new StyleSheet();

var body:Object = new Object();
body.marginRight = 12;
body.marginLeft = 12;

var h1:Object = new Object();
h1.fontWeight = "bold";
h1.color = "#6666CC";
h1.fontSize = 20;

var h2:Object = {fontWeight:"bold",
                  color:"#666CC",
                  fontSize:18
                 }

var a:Object = {color:"#0000FF",
                 textDecoration:"underline"
                }

var aHover:Object = {color:"#0099CC"};
var aVisited:Object = {color:"#000000"};
var leadParagraph = {fontSize:14};

styleSheet.setStyle("h1", h1);
styleSheet.setStyle("h2", h2);
styleSheet.setStyle("a", a);
styleSheet.setStyle("a:hover", aHover);
styleSheet.setStyle("body", body);
styleSheet.setStyle(".leadParagraph", leadParagraph);

txtContent.styleSheet = styleSheet;
```

Code – Example_loadHTML.fla (continued)

```
var urlRequest:URLRequest = new
URLRequest("timesSquare.html");

var urlLoader:URLLoader = new URLLoader(urlRequest);

urlLoader.addEventListener(Event.COMPLETE,
onComplete);

function onComplete(event:Event):void
{
   txtContent.htmlText =

   event.target.data.split("\n").join("");
        scrollBar.update();
}
```

Code – Example_externalCss.fla

```
// Initialize.
var sheet:StyleSheet = new StyleSheet();

// Loaders for HTML and CSS.
var cssRequest:URLRequest = new
URLRequest("css/styles.css");
var cssLoader:URLLoader = new URLLoader();
cssLoader.addEventListener(Event.COMPLETE,
cssLoadedHandler);
cssLoader.load(cssRequest);

var contentRequest:URLRequest = new
URLRequest("timesSquare.html");
var contentLoader:URLLoader = new URLLoader();
contentLoader.addEventListener(Event.COMPLETE,
contentLoadedHandler);
contentLoader.load( contentRequest );

// Handlers for loaders.
function cssLoadedHandler(event:Event):void
{
   sheet.parseCSS(event.target.data);
   txtContent.styleSheet = sheet;
}

function contentLoadedHandler(event:Event):void
{
   txtContent.htmlText =
        event.target.data.split("\n").join("");
   scrollBar.update();
}
```

CHAPTER 10 – FINAL PROJECT

Overview/Challenge

Related file: The following file contains the solution to the final project. [class files]/finalProject/Solution_ichibanTravel.swf.

Open, run and explore the SWF for the solutions file.

Look at the files in the finalProject folder.

Examine the subdirectories and the files inside them.

This is the final project for this course. No new material is presented in this chapter. The challenge is to use ActionScript to assemble a travel company's website with many of the files built during this course. The solution will need just a very few lines of code.

During this course a number of different types of projects have been built. All projects provided solutions to common programming tasks a Flash developer might be expected to perform. All the projects were built using best practices to produce code that is easier to read, understand and maintain.

The purpose of this chapter is to challenge the student to apply what they have learned and create a dynamic Flash application that loads external content. It also provides a chance to build an application using the MVC (Model View Controller) design pattern.

A design pattern is simply a recognized approach to common tasks. The MVC design pattern presents different views of data to a user through the use of a controller.

The controller will be the file created in this chapter. The controller will only hold the background artwork, a buttons group and the ActionScript to load other content. Some content, such as the ad and the slideshow will be loaded once. Other content will be loaded as the user interacts with buttons.

The model will be the information contained in the separate SWFs.

The view will be the SWFs that are presented to the user.

The controller, the main SWF, by itself will be relatively light weight and download quickly, even with the large background artwork. Other content will be loaded as needed, providing a better user experience.

Check out the Next Level chapter for a preview of an advanced way to create the loaders.

Try it – Final project

Challenge

Create a Flash web site using ActionScript, MVC architecture and best practices.

There is a suggestion for solving the challenge on this page. The following page offers a solution. A starter file and content has been provided.

Starter File: [class files]/finalProject/Begin_ichibanTravel.fla.

The starter file has buttons for navigation on stage and areas to load content. Content has already been created from earlier projects in the book. It is in the same directory as the starter file.

The buttons on stage have been named. Sequential naming was used button1, button2, etc.

Suggestions

1. Loaders need to be placed on stage and named.
2. The buttons need to be assembled into a movieClip. The buttons have instance names assigned to them. The movieClip holding the buttons will need the actions to make it work as a button group. This can be copied from any example of an advanced movieClip button group. The group will need an instance name.
3. In the main timeline:
    a. Initialize the buttons. Set their labels and extra info.
    b. Initialize the loaders for ad and slide show. Load both.
    c. Set the first button.
    d. Load the content associated with the first button.
    e. Assign the button group handler.
    f. Write the handler for the button group.

Some extra ideas

Use tweens to fade in the content.

Use a progress bar for the main content.

Use event handling to load the first piece of main content. After the first swf for main content is loaded load the side slide show and bottom ad banner.

No solution is offered here in the book, but you can peek at the solution file: [class files]/finalProject/Solution_ichibanTravel.fla.

Have fun! ☺

SOLUTION –Main timeline code

File[class files]/finalProject/Solution_ichibanTravel.fla.
This file provides a solution for the challenge.

The actions for the navigation button group are on the next page.

In frame 1 of the main timeline.

```
// Initialize the buttons with labels and extra info.
mcNavigation.button1.init("Home","home.swf");
mcNavigation.button2.init("Boston","boston.swf");
mcNavigation.button3.init("Chicago","chicago.swf");
mcNavigation.button4.init("Manhattan","manhattan.swf")
;
mcNavigation.button5.init("San Francisco",
                          "sanFrancisco.swf");
mcNavigation.button6.init("Seattle","seattle.swf");
mcNavigation.button7.init("Where is
that?","game.swf");

// Initialize loaders.
contentLoader.scaleContent = false;
adLoader.scaleContent = false;
rightSideLoader.scaleContent = false;

contentLoader.source = "home.swf";
adLoader.source = "carBanner.swf";
rightSideLoader.source = "sideSlideShow.swf";

// Set the first button.
mcNavigation.setButtons(mcNavigation.button1);
```

Code continues on the next page...

SOLUTION –Main timeline code

```
// Assign handler.
mcNavigation.addEventListener(MouseEvent.CLICK,
                              navigationHandler );


// Handler.
function navigationHandler (event:Event):void
{
   // Set the buttons.
   mcNavigation.setButtons(event.target as MovieClip);
   // Load content.
   contentLoader.source = event.target.extraData;
}
```

The actions for the navigation button group begin on the next page.

SOLUTION – Final project mcNavigation code

In frame 1 of mcNavigation .

This code is 'boilerplate'. It is written without any dependencies its children or its parents. It will be the same in every project.

```
// Create variable to hold...
// ...button that was disabled.
var previousButton:MovieClip;

// Prevent clicks in empty spaces of...
// ...buttonGroup from triggering handler.
mouseEnabled = false;

// Re-enable the disabled button.
// Disable last button selected.
// Called from buttonGroup handler in main timeline.
function setButtons(selectedButton:MovieClip):void
{
   // This if prevents errors the first time...
   // ...toggleButtons is called when...
   // ...there is no previousButton.
   if (previousButton)
   {
        // Enable old button.
        previousButton.gotoAndStop("_up");
   }
   // Disable new button.
   selectedButton.gotoAndStop("_off");
   // Store which button is now disabled.
   previousButton = selectedButton;
}
```

CHAPTER 11 –THE NEXT LEVEL

Congratulations on completing the Introduction to ActionScript course.

Welcome to the next level!

The next course, Advanced ActionScript, shows how to build advanced slide shows, games and animations, work with components, build media players for videos and music and use data to drive your applications.

I would like to offer you a small look at some of the material covered in the Advanced ActionScript book. This example discusses using a more sophisticated approach to create loaders. I hope you enjoy it

Programmatic instantiation

Related file: The following file contains the examples for this discussion. [class files]/nextLevel/Example_loader.fla

In the last chapter loaders were added to the project by physically placing them on the stage. This was a simple, direct and effective approach. The only drawback is that it limits the application to using only the loaders created by physically placing them on the stage.

Larger applications are often driven by XML data and ActionScript. XML data is loaded into a controller (the main SWF). Content is then added from the library, drawn with ActionScript or FXG and/or loaded from external sources. The appearance and function of the application can be changed by editing the XML and making new assets available.

In these applications it is not necessary to physically place objects on the stage. Objects are instantiated and placed on the stage solely with ActionScript. This enables SWF development in tools that do not have a stage and library. This is a common technique used in Flex/Flash Builder development and applications.

Examples in this book have already created objects such as Timers using only ActionScript. Those objects were all intangible. They had no presence on the stage. Using ActionScript to create objects on the stage is similar. It just requires one extra step.

Objects intended for the stage, such as loaders, are created the same way objects like Timers are.

```
var loader:Loader = new Loader();
```

This creates an instance of the Loader class. The Loader class is the class that the UILoader component uses under its hood.

The loader will exist at this point but it will only be in memory. Flash does not know that it should be drawn on the stage. The addChild() method instructs Flash to add the loader to the display list and render it.

```
addChild(loader);
```

Even though Flash is showing the loader on the stage the loader has no content. The Loader class does not have a source property the way the UILoader component did. Content is loaded by sending an URLRequest to the load() method of the Loader class.

```
loader.load(new URLRequest("images/navyPier.jpg"));
```

Positioning and other initialization may also need to be done. The exact order of these tasks after the loader is instantiated does not matter. AddChild is often the last task. This is used as a convention to show that all initialization has been done.

The following is an example of the whole process.

```
var loader:Loader = new Loader();
loader.load(new URLRequest("images/navyPier.jpg"));
loader.x = 50;
loader.y = 50;
addChild(loader);
```

A different solution to the last chapter would not have used the UILoader components. It would have used ActionScript, similar to the above example, to create and populate each loader.

There is a solution file for this technique in the class file's nextLevel folder. This file should be moved to the loadingContent folder to work properly. Students are encouraged to try using this technique to solve the challenge in the previous chapter on Loading Content.

www.ingramcontent.com/pod-product-compliance
Lightning Source LLC
Chambersburg PA
CBHW080408060326
40689CB00019B/4171
* 9 7 8 1 4 6 1 0 1 9 8 5 5 *